UPWARD

STRATEGIES FOR SUCCESS IN BUSINESS, LIFE, AND RELATIONSHIPS

JOHN & JUDY O'LEARY

UPWARD
STRATEGIES FOR SUCCESS IN BUSINESS, LIFE, AND RELATIONSHIPS

Cover design by Kristy Prince

DECAPOLIS
PUBLISHING
A Club 52 Book

www.decapolisbooks.com
www.club52.com
Printed in the United States of America

CONTENTS

PUBLISHER'S NOTE

Welcome to Decapolis Publishing's first Club 52 book—*Upward*—written by John and Judy O'Leary.

What a joy it is for me to introduce John and Judy O'Leary to you. They were among the first who eagerly agreed to help me mentor aspiring millionaires in a group called Club 52, which was established to educate, motivate, inspire, impart, and mentor winners who believe they have the ministry of wealth and who desire to stay connected to the Great Commission. John and Judy have walked beside me all the way. I am so grateful to them.

In life you face challenges on a regular basis. You want simple, workable, proven solutions. Well, here they are from the pens of two amazing upward thinkers—John and Judy O'Leary.

Our chief editor, Joel Kilpatrick, lives and works in California and had never met them. But after reading and working on their manuscript, he sent me a message that simply read, "John and Judy O'Leary sound like real firecrackers."

Firecrackers? Actually, they are "Silver Salutes," "Cherry Bombs," (remember those?) and "Roman Candles" all rolled into one! John and Judy are a powerful, successful couple who have a gift for capturing heavenly realities and bringing them down to earth so you and I can understand them. If you ever have the opportunity to experience their teaching at a live event, you'll discover what I mean.

Creative, caring, dynamic, genuine, and motivational are just a few of the words that come to mind when I think about John and Judy. They inspire and lift you up to a fresh realm of faith. As you read this book, you'll discover the same sense of excitement that students have experienced in their live seminars and conferences.

John is president of O'Leary Paint Company, with headquarters and manufacturing plant in Lansing, Michigan. O'Leary Paint is a fourth-generation, family-owned company for over 100 years. Today, O'Leary Paint manufactures a complete range of premium paints and coatings. John doesn't brag about his products…but I do. O'Leary Paint products are spectacular.

Now get ready for an adventure in problem solving as John and Judy O'Leary take you on a fresh adventure in *Upward*. I'm proud to have John and Judy as dear friends and fellow laborers in bringing an impartation to those called to the ministry of wealth.

Dave Williams
President, Club 52
www.Club52.com

FOREWORD

We are honored to be among the first readers of this book. It is a wonderful feeling to know that our opinion is held in such high regard. Ramona and I take this role quite seriously, simply because we believe that a book should be four things:

1. Workable
2. Enjoyable
3. Practical
4. Inspirational

We both agree...this book hit the nail on the head in all four areas!

We have been testing the principles we found in this book since the day we received it. We have experienced testimony after testimony where we have used this book as a reference point to our growth by:

- Looking for a problem and solving it
- Practicing upward giving

We recently launched a brand new company, Black Network Television, and this book couldn't have come at a more ideal time. It gave us practical solutions to the problems we faced. As a brand new company, the funds are low, the advertising clients are skeptical, we haven't secured a cable deal yet, and even our faith partners may not have total faith in what we are doing…yet!

Thank God for a leader like Pastor Dave Williams, who believes that if God said it, you just need to do it. With all those seeming problems, we are excited that we are making a difference in the world of broadcasting by presenting a positive image of excellence in our community. This book landed in our laps at a time when it could be put to the acid test. Truly, this book is not just a collection of words; it speaks to the heart and soul of the reader.

We both agree that the takeaways are countless. We could go on and on about how we have lived parts of this book over the past few months, but that would be a book in itself.

These are the reasons we believe other readers should invest in this book. John and Judy have just created the first ever "journey book." This is a book that delivers three important elements for which readers search:

- A way out of a problem
- A way up in this journey called life
- A way into God's heart

Michael & Ramona Woods
CEO & CFO
Black Network Television

*"To solve any problem, here are three
questions to ask yourself:
First, what could I do?
Second, what could I read?
And third, who could I ask?"*

Jim Rohn

O'Leary Paint manufactures and retails paint for companies and customers all over Michigan and Indiana. Business isn't our only problem solving endeavor; life itself is all about solving problems.

I KNOW YOUR CALLING—DO YOU?

I own and operate a business that manufactures and retails paint for companies and customers all over Michigan and Indiana. But if my business card were completely accurate it wouldn't read: "John O'Leary, President." It would read: "John O'Leary, Problem Solver."

Why? Because I'm involved in solving problems all day long. "President" is just a fancy way of saying I solve the normal problems that pop up in business life—problems with the supply line, equipment, personnel, management, on the factory floor, and in the business office. I heard one business leader say he manages people who manage people who manage people. I tweak that and say, "I solve problems for people who solve problems for people who solve problems." If I do my job right, it helps people all the way down the line.

Business is, by nature, a problem solving endeavor. Every business is trying to solve a problem people have, or a problem people didn't know they had until they heard the sales pitch. At O'Leary Paint Company, we hope to solve our customers' paint and surface protection problems better than anyone else. I want to effectively remove any paint-related problems from their lives so they don't have to think about them anymore.

If you think about it, owning a business isn't our only problem solving endeavor; life itself is all about solving problems. In fact, if you ever run out of problems to solve, let me know—I want to learn your secret! The truth is, you will never run out. Problems exist for a reason—for us to solve them and move to higher levels in our God-given callings. Every problem on earth is a reward in disguise. Whenever a problem pops up, it is your opportunity to move forward into greater responsibility, maturity, wealth, and influence for the sake of God's Kingdom.

To be effective in every aspect of life—business, personally, and as a follower of Jesus Christ—you must become an effective problem solver.

Can you guess the topic of much of this book?

Solving problems is also critical in your journey to move upward and to becoming wealthy, which is the other important theme of this book. When you have finished, you will be a better problem solver and have the blessing of God on your finances as you put into practice the hard-won advice Judy and I offer in these pages.

So, let's get to it.

"When you confront a problem you begin to solve it."

Rudy Giuliani

John and Judy speaking at Club 52. You are called to be a
problem solver—and to receive rewards!

CHAPTER 1

PRINCIPLES OF PROBLEM SOLVING

There will never be a shortage of problems to solve—not until Jesus comes. Yet some people look at the problems in their personal, professional, and spiritual lives and become overwhelmed and disheartened.

It's time to change that response! You and I can't avoid problems. It's just not possible. Nor can we afford emotional paralysis or hopelessness. No way! Problem solving is our greatest opportunity to reach a higher level in all areas of life. Let me emphasize that so you know how important this statement is:

Problem solving is our greatest opportunity to reach a higher level in all areas of life!

Do you want to move higher in your service to God, your finances, personal life, your parenting, hobbies, and in every other area? Then focus your mind on the fact that rewards are reserved for people who choose to be problem solvers. You are called to be one of them—and you can receive those rewards. Isn't that the best news you've heard all day?

Let me offer some basic ideas inspired by a "wisdom teacher" I really admire—Mike Murdock.[1] I was influenced by his principles when I compiled this list. It re-energizes me every time I read it, which I do regularly when I get knocked around and need to get back on track. These principles will guide us as we learn how to become problem solvers.

1. YOU WERE CREATED TO BE A PROBLEM SOLVER

God is the ultimate problem solver, and we are created in his image and likeness. In fact, the reason you are on the planet is because there is a problem here that only you can solve. Whether you realize it or not, you are on a God-given mission. You have a specific purpose. If you haven't already found problems, you should go looking for them!

It has been this way from the beginning. In Genesis 2:15, God gave Adam a problem to solve: guide, guard, and govern the Garden of Eden. Adam and Eve also solved the population problem by obeying God's command to be fruitful and multiply (fun problem to solve!).

Problem solving permeates humanity's purpose. Think about it—your employer pays you for one reason: you solve a problem—or multiple problems—for him or her. Even your spouse (if you have one) is really drawn to you because you "solve" the gaps in the life you share together. Problem solving is your calling in virtually every area of life.

2. YOUR GIFTS AND SKILLS ARE PROBLEM SOLVING TOOLS

I was at the airport in the dead of winter, and my flight was delayed because the airline ran out of de-icer for the

---

[1] Murdock, Mike, *The Wisdom Commentary of Mike Murdock, Vol. 1*, The Wisdom Center, 4051 Denton Highway, Ft. Worth, TX, 76117, 2003.

plane. When I heard that, a little light bulb went on over my entrepreneurial head. I thought, our paint company uses de-icer. I could sell some to the airport. I spoke to the airport personnel, sold them de-icer, and solved their problem on the spot. I was rewarded with a free flight, an upgrade to first-class, and the esteem of the other people on the plane whose trips I had saved. And if that wasn't enough, I also made a respectable profit.

Wherever you serve—in business, home, or ministry—your skills are your problem solving tools. People need you! They are ready and willing to pay money to have their problems solved.

Who wants to take their own trash to the dump every week? Nobody! We gladly pay someone to solve that problem for us.

Who wants to investigate corruption in politics and business? Not many, so we pay journalists to do that for us.

Who wants to spend the time to become a virtuoso musician or songwriter? Only a few can, and we let them "solve" that problem of our need for entertainment.

Look around you—there are problems everywhere. No matter what you do for a living, you are in the problem solving business.

3. THE SIZE OF THE PROBLEMS YOU SOLVE DETERMINES YOUR EARNINGS

As a business owner, I have learned that the bigger the problem I solve, the bigger the reward I receive. The correlation is obvious. It's why the doctor earns more than the receptionist. It took more hard work and education to become a doctor than it took to become a receptionist. It's more important to prescribe the proper treatment to get you well than to schedule your appointment.

I try to solve the biggest problems I think I can handle. My business won some of our largest accounts by taking on big challenges. For example, we landed the University of Michigan account because neither the university nor our competition wanted to store and dispose of leftover paint. It was a big pain in the neck for them. Nobody wanted to touch the problem. It was too big—too problematic.

But in that problem I saw an opportunity. I offered to pick up the leftover paint from the university every quarter, blend it together and match it so it could be used as primer in their dormitories. The competition chose to cling to their primer sales instead of solving their client's problem. Because I made that offer, something cool happened: We earned the whole University of Michigan account!

Big Problem + Big Solution = Big Reward

David solved King Saul's problem with Goliath (see 1 Samuel 17). The problem was huge, and so was the reward. David got to marry royalty and was exempt from paying taxes. How is that for a reward?

There's no such thing as, "That's not my problem," or "That problem is too big," or "That problem is not worth my time." Every problem is a stepping-stone and an opportunity to attain greater earnings and greater responsibilities—so bring those problems on!

4. RELATIONSHIPS ARE YOUR RESOURCE CENTER FOR PROBLEM SOLVING

My dad is the king of building relationships, and he makes it look easy. He seems to know everyone and everyone seems to know him.

Often, when my brother David and I (we run the company together) are trying to solve a problem, we turn to each other and say, "I wonder who Dad knows that could help us?" That has become the most valuable problem solving phrase in our business.

Relationships are a first resource for solving problems. Here we are with Michael and Ramona Woods and Pastor Dave Williams.

When we were trying to get zoning permission for our paint plant, my Dad knew someone working in city government. Whenever we need a door opened to bid on a job, more often than not, my Dad knows someone who can open that door for us. Relationships that he established in the community afford us opportunities to solve our problems.

Relationships are a first resource for solving problems. Don't look past them, look for them, and you will find a treasure-trove of solutions.

For example, a few years ago, my wife Judy was training a woman to run in her first marathon. As the relationship developed, Judy learned the woman had an autistic child who was being denied a needed kidney transplant because the doctors said his quality of life wouldn't be improved. Judy has a close relationship with one of the longest surviving kidney transplant patients in the country, who is also highly involved in the National Kidney Foundation. Judy connected them, and within one month that autistic child had a new kidney. The relationship connection solved the family's problem...big time!

When you have a large pool of relationships to draw from, you will always end up knowing someone who has an answer. You don't have to know everything about how to solve every problem that arises; you just have to know the right people. Spend time and energy building a community around you. Those relationships will pay off over and over. Someday, you may be fortunate enough to solve their problems.

5. PROBLEM SOLVERS STAND OUT IN A CROWD

My friend, a motivational speaker, once shared with me his biggest challenge. Potential clients always wanted to negotiate a lower fee than the one he advertised—sometimes all the way down to half his normal fee! "It's hard on me," he confided. "Negotiating is not my strong suit."

Together, we devised a plan to address customers who wanted to negotiate his fee, yet allowed him to stand his ground and stay within his comfort zone. We decided to find another motivational speaker who was just starting his career, a speaker who was not as experienced and who was asking a lower fee. The deal was, my friend would agree to recommend him to clients who wanted to pay less, and then collect a finder's fee for every job the less-experienced speaker received through my friend.

Now you are probably thinking, "Are you crazy? Why would he promote someone other than himself?"

Our premise was simple:

- Everyone wants what he or she can't have.
- Nobody wants second best.

He implemented this strategy and started telling potential clients, "My fee is fixed, but I appreciate that you can't afford it. I can recommend a great guy who is more in your price range." Two years and a hundred pitches later, only one client has chosen the less expensive speaker. Why? Because my friend is a proven problem solver. He is worth the money he charges. Everyone wants the top banana. He now tells everyone how promoting someone else advanced his business.

There was an unexpected reward for me in this situation. One man, who heard my friend tell this story, was so impressed with my problem solving suggestion that he got in touch with me and asked me to sit on the board of his company! I was blessed because of the advice I had given to a friend.

Distinguish yourself as a problem solver and people will flock to you. Your value will be recognized, and you will begin to attract success.

6. PROBLEM SOLVERS ATTRACT GREAT PEOPLE

The Bible says:

> **A man's gift makes room for him, and brings him before great men.**
>
> **Proverbs 18:16**

I have seen this happen in our business and in our church. Our pastor, Dave Williams, is a great man. He draws those whom I consider to be great people to him. Because of his leadership, there is a whole community of problem solvers at our church. These people have learned problem solving principles and continue to sharpen each other as iron sharpens iron.

When you become a problem solver, other problem solvers will naturally be attracted to you. This will help you learn and advance more quickly as you gain wisdom and knowledge from them.

7. GOD GRANTS FAVOR TO PROBLEM SOLVERS

Favor flows when we solve a problem for someone. I had a mentor who invested in me and helped me in countless ways. When I was asked to recommend a new board member at the bank board I sit on, this man came to mind. I recommended him, and now he sits on two of their boards, chairs one of them, and is in a paid position of influence. God gave him favor through me because this mentor had helped me to solve many of my problems.

> ...whatever good anyone does, he will receive the same from the Lord....
>
> **Ephesians 6:8 NKJV**

This is a basic life principle: We reap what we sow. Favor flows to problem solvers just as water runs downhill.

8. SOMEONE IS ALWAYS WATCHING

I saw a video of a woman who stopped on the sidewalk to pet a cat. Then she glanced around to see if anyone was watching and promptly threw the cat into a garbage can, closed the lid, and kept walking. Can you imagine? Little did she know there were surveillance cameras on the property.

There was a huge uproar in the community when the video became public, and this woman suffered great embarrassment. I never did hear if the cat was rescued—I sure hope so!

Someone is always watching, even when you don't think so. In this woman's case it was bad news but for problem solvers it's great news! It's an opportunity to shine. Even if you are alone (or think you're alone), God is watching. And it's often the case that other people are watching as well—to see your character in action.

This principle was made very clear to me in 2009. It was a challenging year and, like many other businesses, we faced the prospect of downsizing our staff due to economic conditions. With great difficulty, we determined that 15% of our workforce needed to be laid off. My brother and I split the layoff list and, on one "Black Friday," we went around delivering the bad news. This was one of the worst days in my career.

It was the end of the day, and I was giving notice to the last person on my list—a salesman who had only been with us a short time—and it couldn't have gone worse. He handled himself very poorly. He stomped around and called me every name in the book (and I'm not talking about the Bible). He said it wasn't fair because he out-worked everyone there, and then he stormed out—a terrible end to a terrible day.

As I was looking for our Operations Manager, I spotted a young man who had worked for our company for 12 years; he was busy labeling buckets in the far corner of the building. This surprised me because he was on the layoff list, and I was quite certain my brother had given him the news that morning. I stepped back and called my brother. He confirmed that he had let the man go that morning and, after explaining the layoff compensation, told him he was free to go home right then.

"Well," I said, "He's still here working!" Baffled, I approached the man and asked what he was doing. He barely looked up; he was busy labeling.

"My manager," he explained, "is going to have a huge problem on Monday if I don't get this product labeled."

I said, "Hey, it's a bad day for all of us; why don't you just head home?"

He insisted, "No, I don't want to leave these guys with a problem."

This kid broke my heart! Can you imagine? After 12 years, he had just been told he no longer had a job, and his biggest concern was not himself but his coworkers and our paint company. He, of all people, could have been justified in stomping around yelling, but his servant's heart would not allow it.

I believe God made sure that I saw this kid's heart for our company. He was willing to help with our small problems, even though he was facing a large one. Right then, I purposed in my heart that he would be the first one called back to work, and I'm happy to report that two weeks later he was back with us. Remember, someone is always watching.

Purpose in your heart to be the problem solver God created you to be. It will lead you to great rewards, which is the subject of the next chapter.

"Problems are only opportunities in work clothes"

Henry J. Kaiser

Goal-setting, mentors, losing battles to win wars,
learning to serve from the heart, interviewing well,
and missile lock—it all works!

CHAPTER 2

MILLIONAIRE PRINCIPLES

Our pastor, Dave Williams, has an anointing to create millionaires out of ordinary people. I have seen it happen. I have also observed millionaire business people supercharge their businesses with a few practical and spiritual principles. I'm going to share my top six. If these seem familiar to you, just remember—they have worked for me and for countless others as we chart the path toward greater wealth and influence for the Kingdom's sake. Remember, don't ignore the basics!

1. GOAL SETTING

Goal setting is where all lasting success begins. A few years ago, I was sitting in church listening to Pastor Dave preach on the subject of setting faith goals. He challenged us: "If I come out into the congregation and ask you what your goals and dreams are, can you articulate them to me? Are they written down? Are they specific and measurable? Don't give me a 'Miss America' answer like, 'I'm hoping for world peace'!"

Pastor Dave teaches the importance of setting Faith Goals.

At that moment, I mentally stumbled through my goals, which suddenly seemed vague and poorly formulated, even to me. I realized Pastor Dave was absolutely right. If my goals aren't clear in my mind and I can't state them clearly to others, I do not have goals. This principle came alive to me that day, and I purposed in my heart to put my goals in writing, clearly and specifically.

A major cause of failure in life is an unwillingness to be specific about goals. Goal setting sets your dreams in motion. I have read that putting your goals in writing triples your chances of attaining them—and I believe the percentage is actually even higher than that.

Goal setting is like taking a boat onto a lake. Imagine if you simply put the boat in the water and let it drift. You don't turn on the motor, don't steer it, and don't have a destination in mind. You have no maps or timetable for returning. You just go where the current takes you—probably right back to shore. That's what living without goals is like.

Having goals, on the other hand, is like turning the motor on and heading right to where you've marked on the map you want to go. You do it efficiently and with expectation and joy. Goals energize life and infuse it with meaning, purpose—and success.

After that teaching from Pastor Dave, I started writing down goals for my business. I noticed right away that goal setting helped bring focus and clarity to my work and kept me headed in the right direction. With practice, I've become more and more specific with my goals. For example, I used to write on my list, "I'd like my business to be profitable." But that's pretty vague. What if I made only one dollar of profit? Would I be satisfied? Of course not! I needed to be more specific.

So I did a little research and found out what the best companies in my field are making in profit—about ten percent after taxes. I changed my goal to: "I want to make ten percent profit after taxes." See the difference? One goal was general and one was specific. One was a light bulb, and one was a laser beam.

Now I'm a devoted goal-setter. I get specific about my finances, marriage, family, health, and spiritual life. I'm here to tell you, goal-setting works! And I've learned the secret to super-charging my goals…I share them with other people—not with just anybody but with people who support my vision. The Bible says that iron sharpens iron. When I share my goals I set myself up for accountability, guidance, and support. I also put healthy expectations on myself. Once I put it out there, I'm a lot more likely to achieve it.

I was talking about goals with some friends a few years ago, and we decided to get together regularly to discuss our progress and pitfalls with the idea of helping each other reach our goals. We named our group "The Goal Guys." Four times a year, we meet over breakfast and distribute copies of our goals. We make suggestions, ask questions, offer assistance, and pool our resources. Talk about motivation! There's no way I want to show up without making progress. I want to encourage everyone: get specific, write your goals down, and get yourself into a community where people are watching to see if you reach them. It will change your life!

Goal Guys: Chris Johnson, Rick Norris, Kirk Mansberger, & John O'Leary

2. MENTORS

I'm convinced that any success I achieve is a direct result of the mentors in my life. I'm not particularly bright, but I have been blessed by choosing good mentors to help me.

I have found two ways to receive wisdom: through my own mistakes and by seeking the wisdom of mentors. The mentor has already walked the path, knows the twists and turns, and can help you navigate them. If you find yourself learning from more than your fair share of mistakes, maybe you need a mentor to help you avoid some of those traps.

The mentor relationship is purposeful. There is an agenda and accountability. A mentor is not a buddy or friend; he is a coach. His purpose is to help identify and strengthen your weaknesses.

My first mentor was my father. He owned our family business before my brother and I took over. He always shared his vision openly and included us in the inner workings of the company. He taught by example.

Once we were in a real estate closing for the purchase of a building. In the middle of the closing—with the owners, the real estate agents, and the attorneys all gathered together—the owners decided to renegotiate the deal. It was an inappropriate, strong-arm tactic. We went back and forth with them for a while until my father stood up, banged his hands on the table, and declared, "That's enough! I have a check in my pocket for the agreed-upon amount. I'll be in the hallway for five minutes. After that, I am going home with my check and the deal is over. You decide." He marched out of the room!

My brother and I followed him out like baby chicks. Once we were in the hallway, we tried to reason with Dad. "We really want this building," we urged. But he interrupted, "Stop! Never be afraid to walk away from a deal." Within five minutes the owners closed the deal at the original terms. What a lesson I learned that day.

Twelve years later, my brother and I were at our own closing and the same thing happened. The buyers attempted to adjust the sale price at the last minute. The attorneys began to debate, and it looked like everything was bogging down. I turned to my brother. He had a look in his eye. I jumped to my feet, banged my hands on the table, and said, "That's enough! I have a check in my pocket for the agreed-upon amount. We'll be in the hallway for five minutes. Then the two of us are going home with our check, and the deal is over. You decide." We marched out of the room.

Once in the hallway, my brother punched me in the arm and said, "I was just about to do that!" We had a good laugh, and soon the buyers came to their senses and we closed the deal.

Thanks, Dad!

I still have mentors, three of them, who guide me through the paths and seasons of my life. They challenge me and expand my vision. With their help, the traps and snares are illuminated and I see new heights. I never miss an opportunity to spend time with these men. They are God-ordained relationships for me.

When considering a mentor, it's important to understand your part as the protégé; you are there to seek direction and learn. This requires a teachable heart. You have to be committed to stay and not leave the relationship when your mentor corrects or admonishes you.

Also, it is the job of the protégé to pursue the mentor. Remember that mentors aren't there to do the work for you. You are there to seek what they've learned not what they've earned. Pray about it, identify some mentors, and then pursue those relationships. You'll supercharge your life.

3. LOSING A BATTLE TO WIN THE WAR

It's easy to fixate on winning immediate conflicts and become shortsighted about what really matters. Here's another secret of success; be willing to give up a battle to win a war.

In Matthew, Jesus said:

> [53] "Don't you realize that I could ask my Father for thousands of angels to protect us, and he would send them instantly?
>
> [54] "But if I did, how would the Scriptures be fulfilled that describe what must happen now?"
>
> **Matthew 26:53–54**

By going to the cross, Jesus laid down his life for our salvation. He gave up the battle to win the war. So should we. It's hard to lay down your rights and accept seeming "failure." However, it's often not a failure at all but a stepping stone to greater victory.

One time, an older couple hired one of our designers and then insisted on ordering an exotic wood floor, even though our designer strongly advised against it. The style of their house was not conducive to this type of floor, but they insisted—so we installed it. Sure enough, they were unhappy with the floor—and refused to pay for it. We sent the manufacturer of the product and the installers to their home, but we could not make them happy. Although it was an expensive, high-end floor, I not only absorbed the cost of the floor, I paid to have it ripped out and then installed a different floor. My workers were upset with me for giving away so much material and labor. The couple had been warned repeatedly about the problems that would result from choosing the floor they insisted they wanted. My employees wanted me to stand firm.

But I looked at the long term. Instead of winning the battle, I decided to try to win the war. I laid my rights down. And because I did, I've gotten more business and positive advertising from this couple. They are influential in the community and tell everyone they know to use our business. We lost that battle, no question about it, but we won the war!

In a conversation with another customer (one of my contractors), he mentioned that business was going well, but he had been burned by one of his developers. "He owes me $80,000, and I had to get my attorney involved," this contractor told me. "My attorney told me he could collect $60,000, but the rest would cost more to fight for than it's worth. So I'm settling for a loss." When we hung up the phone, God put this man's problem on my heart, so I pulled up his account. What a great customer he was! He had bought all the paint for this project from us and paid for it within thirty days, yet he was going to take a $20,000 loss on the project.

I called him back and asked him what percentage of the $20,000 loss was the paint cost on that project? "A little over 20 percent," he answered.

"Okay, I'm going to credit that 20 percent to your account," I told him. The phone went silent. "Are you there?" I asked.

"I gotta go!" he said and abruptly hung up. He was too choked up to speak! He called back a few minutes later and said, "I just have to tell you no one has ever done anything like that for me. You supported me when I hadn't even asked for help." His voice cracked and he quickly hung up again.

I took a loss for this guy to cement our relationship, and now he is our most loyal contractor. If a potential client won't use our paint, he turns the job down!

One last example: A major problem occurred a couple of years ago with our largest industrial account. It was an expensive fix. Their assembly line broke, and there was much debate about who was responsible. They narrowed it down to three paint manufacturers, and even though we weren't convinced we had created the problem, we decided to step up and pay for their assembly line repairs. It was a six-figure hit to our bottom line, causing a quarter of our yearly profit to vanish. The other two manufacturers ran for cover—neither one would pay a cent. They both did the "corporate salute" and blamed everyone else.

It was a tough battle to lose, but in the last few years that account has tripled in size. It's so enormous that, at one point, big national companies descended on this company like vultures to try to take the account away from us. They claimed we were too small to serve a business that size. It is true that we are a regional company without the high profile of a national company. To add insult to injury, the lower management of this business tried to sway upper management against us. But when we all met, upper management declared, "We are not changing suppliers. O'Leary Paint stepped up when no one else would. We won't forget that." Hallelujah! We kept that account because we had been willing to lose a battle earlier.

Every time I give up the battle, I win the war. It's the same pattern of success Jesus showed us at the cross—and it works in everyday life.

4. LEARN TO SERVE BEFORE YOU LEAD

It was my father's company, but as a teenager I cleaned bathrooms, worked in the warehouse, the paint plant, the stores, and drove a truck. I worked under many different managers long before I was given any authority. It's critical to learn to serve under someone before you lead others. Leadership is really about serving. Now I am president and owner of that same company.

One day, Judy heard that Pastor Dave's son, David, needed a summer job during his break from college, so she asked me to hire him. I interviewed David. He is a rock-solid young guy with a servant's heart. That night over dinner Judy asked, "Well, how did it go with David? Did you hire him?"

"Yes, I gave him a job in our paint plant," I answered. "He starts Monday."

"Not the paint plant!" Judy cried. "Isn't there anything in the office for him?"

"Something more comfortable and cushy, you mean?" I asked. "Maybe vice president for the summer?"

She knew what I meant. As tough as it seems, the best way to learn leadership is by learning to serve. David did a great job in the paint plant, and I know he'll go on to great things in whatever career he chooses.

Some people start at the bottom and never work their way up. Why? Because they don't learn to serve, they just learn to comply. While working your way up, it's important to do more than expected and ask for guidance and correction from those above you. In other words, you must develop the heart of a servant.

A good example of this is a young man who started working for us in the warehouse. His goal was to work his way up to an outside sales position. When a position opened up he excitedly interviewed for it, but I decided to hire an experienced outside person. Soon after receiving this disappointing news, he requested a meeting with me. I thought I knew exactly how the meeting would go. He would tell me how it wasn't fair, how he'd paid his dues, and I did him wrong.

I was amazed when the first thing he said was, "It's obvious I didn't get the job because you perceive I'm lacking in some area. I'm ready to do everything you ask of me so the next time a sales job opens, you're only going to think of one person—me. Tell me what skills I lack and who you want me to work under, and I'll do it." His stock went up ten points with me right then. He was promoted the next time a sales position opened up and is currently ranked number three in sales.

One last thing on serving: We are all servants. God is our CEO. In fact, at our company I decided years ago to name

God as our CEO. The flow chart puts my name under his. I love this visual reminder that I, too, am in the position of servant. I don't have to rely on my own understanding or limited natural talents. With God in charge, no weapon formed against our company will prosper. I sleep a lot better at night with him in charge.

5. HONE YOUR INTERVIEW SKILLS

My company has the top twelve salesmen in the state of Michigan, and there's one reason for it: I know I'm not the smartest guy in the room, so I need to surround myself with smart guys. I have learned the valuable skill of recognizing the best and the brightest from all the rest.

There is a science, even an art, to interviewing and being interviewed. Whether you are running a company or looking to advance, interviewing and being interviewed well is essential to success. It also determines the success or failure of your company, because no company is better than its people. There are many books and resources about how to interview people effectively and how to be an effective interviewee. I recommend reading everything you can get your hands on.

6. MISSILE LOCK

"Missile Lock" is a guidance system used by the military to hit targets. Once missile lock latches onto a target, it ignores all other options and pursues the target until it makes a hit.

In the same way, you can lock on to a goal and not let go until the objective is met. You don't consider the economy, the circumstances, or the critics who say it can't be done. Missile Lock is the moment in life when you declare, "That will be mine!"

Our daughter (Mini-Me) graduated from University of Michigan with a teaching degree. Because she graduated in December, and teaching jobs don't begin until August, she told us she had decided to spend the winter in Hawaii.

Hawaii?

After our daughter graduated from University of Michigan with a teaching degree, she was able to spend the winter in Hawaii.

We wondered how she would pull it off, considering that if you could go around the world on a dime, she couldn't even get out of sight. But guess what happened? She used her missile lock and found a way. She contacted an organic farm in Hawaii and volunteered to be an intern for them in exchange for room and board. When we went to Hawaii as a family over Christmas, we came home and she stayed. She lived there all winter in tropical bliss.

That's missile lock! You see it all the time in extraordinary people who experience the kind of adversity that would take the average person down. You see it in elite athletes and people at the top of their professions. With missile lock there is no second-guessing. The Bible says double-minded people won't receive anything.

> **But when you ask him, be sure that your faith is in God alone. Do not waver, for a person with divided loyalty is as unsettled as a wave of the sea that is blown and tossed by the wind.**
>
> **James 1:6**

Set the goal, commit to it, stay focused, and you will attain it.

During the fourth year of manufacturing paint in our own plant, we bid on a job at Oldsmobile for 50,000 gallons of paint. The bid was bigger than any job we had ever done, but I thought we could do it—somehow. Our management team disagreed and tried to convince me not to bid for the job, but I did it anyway. I had fixed on the goal of getting this bid and doing a great job on it.

We won the bid, and I worked in the factory every night, running a crew to make the extra paint. For four months we made 2,000 extra gallons of paint per day, managing to stay ahead of the order. There was continual adversity—broken pumps, container shortages. One night I had to get into the vat of paint up to my hips to fill buckets by hand. At the end of the deal, we sold not 50,000 gallons but 80,000 gallons to Oldsmobile because we took hold of that goal and never let go. Missile Lock.

I'm sure you're tenacious at times and have your own version of missile lock, but let me mention three components that, in my experience, are always part of it:

1. Write down your desire. Pastor Dave says, "Don't just think it; INK it!"

2. Speak out your desire. Make it audible to yourself and others. Declare what you want, not what you presently see in the natural. Use your imagination to make a mental picture of your desire coming to pass. Desire defies logic!

3. Keep speaking your desire, envisioning it, and working for it until it happens.

We've talked about goal-setting, having mentors, losing battles to win wars, learning to serve from the heart, interviewing well, and missile lock—yet, you may still be asking yourself, "Does this stuff really work in everyday life?" I'll answer that with my own question, "If it doesn't work, how does a guy like me land a smart, smokin' hot wife like Judy?" Speaking of whom, she wrote the next couple of chapters. Enjoy!

"There are very few personal problems that cannot be solved through a suitable application of high explosives."

Scott Adams (Dilbert)

Our daughter, Amber, and son-in-law, JD.
God is a family man, and we are that family.

CHAPTER 3

WHEN GOD BECOMES YOUR PROBLEM SOLVER

I used my missile lock to get John to marry me! He is the love of my life.

Everything you've read in the previous chapters actually happened. I was there and, if I had a thousand pages, I could add many other stories and examples of how these principles work in everyday life. Now I want to turn the subject around and address the fact that when you become a problem solver, God will solve your problems! It really is an amazing fact: The more you help others solve their problems, the more God will solve yours.

Regrettably, many Christians don't know how to let God solve their problems. They have not learned how to receive God's blessings. It is a learned skill I want to teach in this chapter.

First, a story: I was at a prayer meeting with other women, and we were taking turns praying. When a woman named Kathy began praying, I heard her speak the most beautiful words of love to God. I couldn't believe my ears! I had never heard anything like it. After the meeting, to my amazement, Kathy began to tell me how she had lost her husband, her home, her health, and was one step away from living on the street.

It struck me—how could this woman who has such a strong, loving relationship with God be in this condition?

Kathy was apparently thinking the same thing. She later told me that she asked, "God, I love you, but I'm broke, busted, and disgusted. Why am I not blessed financially?" God answered with the most profound statement: "Yes, you have figured out how to love me, but you have not figured out how to let me love you."

It doesn't matter how much we love God—we have to complete the circle by letting him love us in return. This means getting to know him as Father, not just as "boss" or "master." If we only know him as God, we will never move from "servant" mentality to becoming his son or daughter. Remember the Gospel tells us:

> **"But as many as *received* Him, to them He gave the right to become children of God...."**
> **John 1:12a NKJV, italics added**

We are children of God! Not just followers or servants, but children.

In Romans, the Word tells us we should not be like cowering, fearful slaves. We should behave instead like God's very own children, adopted into his family, calling him Father, dear Father.

> **[16] For his Spirit joins with our spirit to affirm that we are God's children.**

[17] **And since we are his children, we are his heirs. In fact, together with Christ we are heirs of God's glory.**

Romans 8:16–17a

GETTING TO KNOW "DAD"

I don't know about you, but I always used to address God as "God" in my prayer time. Then one day I had a supernatural revelation. I realized I had earned the privilege and right to call God "Dad" on the day I was born again. He spoke to my heart and said, "Will you please start using your rights?"

God longs to be called Father, Dad, or Daddy. He longs for greater intimacy with us. As he says in Jeremiah:

> **"I thought to myself, 'I would love to treat you as my own children!' I wanted nothing more than to give you this beautiful land—the finest possession in the world. *I looked forward to your calling me 'Father,'* and I wanted you never to turn from me."**
>
> **Jeremiah 3:19, italics added**

God didn't send his Son to die so he could have employees! He wanted children. God is a family man, and we are that family. We don't always have to be so formal. Can you imagine one of your hungry children popping into the kitchen and saying, "My mother, who art in the kitchen, give me this day my daily bread"? No! Children say, "Hey, Mom, what's to eat around here?"

Believe it or not, that's how I talk to God now. I don't storm the gates of heaven, because the Word says Jesus is as close as my heart. My time with my Dad is intimate. Once I understood this, I stopped seeking that great God in the sky—distant and remote. Luke declares that the kingdom of God is within you.

"nor will they say, 'See here!' or 'See there!' For indeed, the kingdom of God is within you."

Luke 17:21 NKJV

That's closeness. Some people have a hard time believing this is an appropriate relationship. But God invites us to be his children. He loves us like a Father! It's mind-boggling.

Have you ever noticed that the more something costs the more people value it? Well, God paid the highest price for you—the shed blood of his only Son. God isn't merely tolerating you, and he didn't pay that high price so he could jerk you around and make it hard for you to find him. He wants to be found by you, because he loves you. You are his treasured possession. He sacrificed Jesus, his only child, to have many, many children—like you and me.

The other day, a woman told me, "I've been serving God my whole life; I don't know why I've had nothing but suffering." Could it be because God isn't looking for servants? He already has servants—they're called angels. What he wants are sons and daughters.

In the story of the prodigal son, Jesus tells of two sons with two different relationships with their father: a "good" son and a "bad" son.

[11] To illustrate the point further, Jesus told them this story: "A man had two sons.

[12] "The younger son told his father, 'I want my share of your estate now before you die.' So his father agreed to divide his wealth between his sons.

[13] "A few days later this younger son packed all his belongings and moved to a distant land, and there he wasted all his money in wild living.

[14] "About the time his money ran out, a great famine swept over the land, and he began to starve.

¹⁵ "He persuaded a local farmer to hire him, and the man sent him into his fields to feed the pigs.

¹⁶ "The young man became so hungry that even the pods he was feeding the pigs looked good to him. But no one gave him anything.

¹⁷ "When he finally came to his senses, he said to himself, 'At home even the hired servants have food enough to spare, and here I am dying of hunger!

¹⁸ "I will go home to my father and say, 'Father, I have sinned against both heaven and you,

¹⁹ 'and I am no longer worthy of being called your son. Please take me on as a hired servant.'

²⁰ "So he returned home to his father. And while he was still a long way off, his father saw him coming. Filled with love and compassion, he ran to his son, embraced him, and kissed him.

²¹ "His son said to him, 'Father, I have sinned against both heaven and you, and I am no longer worthy of being called your son.'

²² "But his father said to the servants, 'Quick! Bring the finest robe in the house and put it on him. Get a ring for his finger and sandals for his feet.

²³ "And kill the calf we have been fattening. We must celebrate with a feast,

²⁴ "'for this son of mine was dead and has now returned to life. He was lost, but now he is found.' So the party began.

²⁵ "Meanwhile, the older son was in the fields working. When he returned home, he heard music and dancing in the house,

²⁶ "and he asked one of the servants what was going on.

²⁷ "'Your brother is back,' he was told, 'and your father has killed the fattened calf. We are celebrating because of his safe return.'

²⁸ "The older brother was angry and wouldn't go in. His father came out and begged him,

²⁹ "but he replied, 'All these years I've slaved for you and never once refused to do a single thing you told me to. And in all that time you never gave me even one young goat for a feast with my friends.

³⁰ "'Yet when this son of yours comes back after squandering your money on prostitutes, you celebrate by killing the fattened calf!'

³¹ "His father said to him, 'Look, dear son, you have always stayed by me, and everything I have is yours.

³² "We had to celebrate this happy day. For your brother was dead and has come back to life! He was lost, but now he is found!'"

Luke 15:11–32

The good son stayed with the father, while the prodigal son received his inheritance and ran away and wasted it in riotous living. The good son had a servant's mentality. Even though he lived in his father's house, he behaved like a servant. He thought he could earn his father's regard through serving or being good. He thought wrong! He never even got a young goat to slaughter and eat with his friends—even though everything his father owned was his as well.

Many people see the foolishness of the wasteful son, but the good son was even less mature and less intelligent than the prodigal son. The good son represents many people today who are living in self-imposed bondage that our Father never envisioned for them. Trying to earn his father's favor didn't work for the good son, and it won't work for us.

The prodigal son, on the other hand, was a brat. He ran off with his share of the inheritance and wasted it. And when he realized he was in trouble, he ran home to daddy. His father saw him from a distance and what did he do? He ran to him! This is the only Bible account of a father running—and he's running to embrace a "bad" son, to restore him and lavish him with abundance that his son hadn't earned or deserved.

I identify with that son. In fact, I'm the brat in the prodigal son story. I've gotten to know God as Father by getting into lots of trouble. The Bible says God is an ever-present help in times of trouble, and I have met him there many times. And you know what? He never once smacked me down lower. Every time I ran to God, he picked me up and set me in a high place. My pastor calls him "The Trouble Untangler." I'm so glad that's who God is, because getting into trouble is my special gift!

Here is one example. Every month, my husband John gives me a paycheck, a generous amount of money that I can use however I want. In exchange, I don't ask for money when I want to buy things.

One particular month, I was planning to fly to Oklahoma to visit my son; I'd be staying four nights in a hotel. I only had $100 left from the paycheck I had received just a few days earlier. I didn't have the nerve to ask John for more money. I was in trouble—and it was trouble I brought on myself! I didn't earn or deserve God's help, but he's my Dad, and he promised to help me in times of trouble. So I ran to him, figuratively climbed onto his lap and said, "Dad! I spent all my money! What should I do?"

I heard him speak to my heart, "I will see that you are taken care of."

I asked, "Should I activate a credit card?"

He replied, "If you do, you'll need it!" He meant that I could trust in him or trust the credit card. Proverbs says:

Trust in your money and down you go!
Proverbs 11:28a

Yikes! I didn't want that; I chose to trust in God.

Now I had a promise; my Dad said he would take care of me. The day of my flight arrived, and I wasn't taken care of yet. John took me to the airport and dropped me off without saying a word about money. I was holding onto God's word to me, but at the same time it wasn't looking good! I nervously looked around to see if anyone was reaching for his wallet but no one was. So, I checked my bag and began walking toward security. Suddenly, my cell phone rang. It was John. "I was thinking," he said, "I bet you don't have enough money. I'm turning around. Meet me out front in three minutes."

He gave me plenty of money and his credit card. It was a great trip, and I had a blast.

This was a win-win-win situation. John got to be the hero (Oh, how I thanked him! I told him he was the best husband on the planet). God got the glory, because it was God who turned John around. I got the money—and the testimony!

Best of all, this incident reaffirmed once again that God is my source! The Bible says over and over, "They cried out to God in their time of trouble, and he delivered them." That's my Dad!

A servant would never run to God for mercy in times of trouble; a servant would try to earn God's blessing. We can't! If we could earn it, then Jesus would have died in vain. And if God let us earn it, he would be saying that there is more than one way to come to him. When Jesus said, "No one can come to the Father except through me," (John 14:6) he meant through grace, and undeserved favor—never by human effort. He said in the Gospel of John:

> **The Spirit alone gives eternal life. Human effort accomplishes nothing.**
>
> **John 6:63a**

He went so far as to say if you try to come in on your own, you are a thief and a robber:

> "I tell you the truth, anyone who sneaks over the wall of a sheepfold, rather than going through the gate, must surely be a thief and a robber!"
>
> **John 10:1**

I love the fact that Jesus didn't come for those who think they are good enough (like the good son); he came for those who know they need him.

The Bible story of Mary and Martha is a parallel to the good son and the prodigal son. Martha was a servant (she had an earning mentality), while Mary just wanted to be with Jesus. Martha was worried about serving the food, while Mary sat at the feet of Jesus. In Luke, Scripture shows how Martha resented Mary and complained about her, just the same way the good son complained about the prodigal son.

> **40** But Martha was distracted by the big dinner she was preparing. She came to Jesus and said, "Lord, doesn't it seem unfair to you that my sister just sits here while I do all the work? Tell her to come and help me."
>
> **41** But the Lord said to her, "My dear Martha, you are worried and upset over all these details!
>
> **42** "There is only one thing worth being concerned about. Mary has discovered it, and it will not be taken away from her."
>
> **Luke 10:40–42**

Jesus basically told Martha, "The problem is, you don't get what's important here, but Mary does."

The one thing worth being concerned about wasn't serving! If Martha had sat at Jesus' feet with Mary instead of being so busy, maybe Jesus would've done what he did with the bread and fish—multiplied them. The best part is there would be no slaving in the kitchen! If we let him be Lord, he'll take care of us. That's the lesson of that story.

John and our daughter at her dream wedding. If we, being human, know how to give good gifts to our children, how much more! What do you want from your Dad? Ask him! He wants to bless you.

Once, I was praying about what I should concentrate on for my spiritual growth. I was thinking of all the things I could change about myself, and got busy assembling a long list, when my Father interrupted, "I have a request. I want you to focus only on one thing and let any other things go."

I asked, "What is it, Dad? What is the one thing?"

I heard that still, small voice say, "Will you spend more time with me?"

I laughed out loud, and I told him, "You must really be desperate to want to spend your time hanging around me!" I felt his answer…"I am desperate—desperate to love you."

His answer wasn't only directed at me; he says the same thing right now to you. Oh, how he loves you!

Have you found the "one needful thing"? It's never too late. God doesn't want you to try to earn his love by serving him. When you try to earn it, you block it from coming. Your goodness is nothing but a filthy rag to God (Isaiah 64:6). Your job is to receive.

GETTING WHAT YOU ASK FOR

I said yes to God's request and began spending more time with him. As I was sitting there at his feet that first day, I said, "I'm running out of things to talk about with you."

His voiced quickened within me, "Ask me questions!"

I thought for a minute and nothing came to mind. So I said half-jokingly, "Can I have a convertible?"

A few weeks later, I heard the back door open. I went into the kitchen and there was John. He didn't say a word but held up a set of keys. I grabbed them, opened the door—and there was a new black convertible Audi TT, exactly like the one I told God I wanted. It even had baseball stitching on the upholstery!

Matthew says:

> **"So if you sinful people know how to give good gifts to your children, *how much more* will your heavenly Father give good gifts to those who ask Him."**
> **Matthew 7:11, italics added**

I like that part—"how much more…." In turn, I handed the keys to my little red sports car to my son, CJ. If we, being human, know how to give good gifts to our children, HOW MUCH MORE!

John later went to the car dealership to get our daughter and son-in-law a new car for their wedding present. The dealer had such a good deal on G6 leases that John came away with three of them—one for each of the kids.

Gabby, my little "Miss you!" girl.

If we, being human, know how to give good gifts to our children, HOW MUCH MORE!

When our daughter, Amber, was pregnant, she was living across the country in a new city and couldn't have a proper baby shower. So we told her to go shopping and pick out everything her heart desired for that baby, and John and I paid for it. If we, being human, know how to give good gifts to our children, HOW MUCH MORE!

There's a little girl in my family (my niece's daughter, Gabby) who has captured my heart. This little one is quite taken with me. She clings to me the entire time I'm with her.

Well, a few months before she turned two, they moved to Chicago. I didn't see her for a couple of months, and during that time she learned to talk. Right before her second birthday, I went to visit her, and I was hoping she'd still remember me because at that young age you never know.

When she saw me, she lunged at my neck and hugged me so tightly while patting my back with her little hand. She kept repeating over and over, "Miss you; miss you; miss you."

Well, my heart melted. I laid awake that night trying to think of a way to really bless that kid. Her birthday was a week later, and I bought her an expensive toy. I could not restrain myself! If we, being human, know how to give good gifts to our children, HOW MUCH MORE!

RECEIVING WELL

Have you ever met someone who doesn't know how to receive a gift? I have. Once, I was riding in my cleaning woman's car, and I offered to fill up her gas tank for her. She wouldn't let me! She was unable to receive this simple gift. I recalled her once telling me, "God has helped you so many times and so many ways. I am a Christian, too, and I can't think of one time God has blessed me." I was speechless; I know God doesn't play favorites. So why were our experiences so different? When I got home I asked God, "Won't you bless her?"

I heard him ask, "When you offered to fill her car with gas, how did that go for you?"

I replied, "She wouldn't let me."

"Well, she won't let me, either," he answered.

Jesus once said:

> **"How often I have wanted to gather Your children together as a hen protects her chicks beneath her wings, *but you wouldn't let Me.*"**
>
> **Matthew 23:37b, italics added**

Receiving does not come naturally to many people. It's an age-old problem; long ago the Apostle Paul struggled with people who couldn't receive. In his letter to the Romans he wrote:

> **"Pray also that the believers there *will be willing to accept* the donation I am taking to Jerusalem."**
>
> **Romans 15:31b, italics added**

It was true then, and it's still true today. Some people just can't receive. The Bible says in Luke:

> **"Give, and you will receive. Your gift will return to you in full—pressed down, shaken together to make room for more, running over, and poured into your lap. The amount you give will determine the amount you get back."**
>
> **Luke 6:38**

In the King James Version, it ends by saying, "shall men give into your bosom." It's a basic skill of the Christian life to graciously receive from the hands of men. God uses the hands of men to bless us. It was God who desired to bless my house-keeper through my hands with a tank of gas, but she refused to receive it. She even concluded, "God must hate me."

In Deuteronomy 1:19–27, we see twelve spies go into the land promised to Israel, and ten of them are unable to receive the blessing! Strangely, they concluded with the same phrase my housekeeper did: "The Lord must hate us." Then they murmured and complained and refused to possess what God already promised them.

> **26 "Nevertheless you would not go up, but rebelled against the command of the LORD your God;**
>
> **27 "and you complained in your tents, and said, *'Because the LORD hates us*, He has brought us out**

of the land of Egypt to deliver us into the hand of the Amorites, to destroy us.' "

Deuteronomy 1:26–27, NKJV italics added

If you don't believe God loves you, you will tolerate living in lack. You will push away what God wants you to have. It's time for us to take our rightful place in God's family. God doesn't bless us because we're good; he blesses us because he is good! He blesses you because you are precious to him; he made you, and he adores you. He blesses you because he loves you. Your part is simple—just spend time with him. In the next chapter, we'll talk about giving effectively, another skill many Christians need to learn.

God is the true source of blessings in our family.
He wants to bless you too.

Grandson Milo…God's answered prayer for our family.

CHAPTER

MASTERING GOD'S
SEED PRINCIPLE

Have you ever known someone who is really good at confessing Scripture, but they never see the promises manifest? They know all the right verses to quote and speak out with confidence, but they always seem to live in lack.

When you see someone living in lack the reason is often that they have not planted any seed. They are standing over the soil and speaking to it in faith, but nothing has been planted. There is nothing for the Word to water.

Get this into your mind: *God responds to seed—not need*. If he responded to need, he would never leave India or Haiti or Africa. God is seed-focused not need-focused. So we must be seed-focused too.

In Mark, chapter four, Jesus taught about sowing and reaping, the seed and the soil.

> ³ **"Listen! A farmer went out to plant some seed.**
>
> ⁴ **"As he scattered it across his field, some of the seed fell on a footpath, and the birds came and ate it.**

⁵ "Other seed fell on shallow soil with underlying rock. The seed sprouted quickly because the soil was shallow.

⁶ "But the plant soon wilted under the hot sun, and since it didn't have deep roots, it died.

⁷ "Other seed fell among thorns that grew up and choked out the tender plants so they produced no grain.

⁸ "Still other seeds fell on fertile soil, and they sprouted, grew, and produced a crop that was thirty, sixty, and even a hundred times as much as had been planted!"

⁹ Then he said, "Anyone with ears to hear should listen and understand."

Mark 4:3–9

Afterward, the disciples approached him and confessed they did not understand. Jesus answered:

"If you can't understand the meaning of this parable, how will you understand all the other parables?"

Mark 4:13b

You must understand this parable to understand every other teaching Jesus gave, because the entire Kingdom of God is based on the seed principle. I repeat; *the entire Kingdom of God is based on the seed principle*. He concluded this parable by saying, "Anyone with ears to hear should listen and understand." Jesus' statement reminds me of when my high school teacher would say, "This is going to be on the test." I would always take special note of what was said next. Jesus was letting us know how important this principle is. The seed principle is on the test! The seed principle is so important, one of the first things God did was to establish it. Following, you will find seven basic truths that will help you understand and master God's seed principle.

¹¹ Then God said, "Let the land sprout with vegetation—every sort of seed-bearing plant, and trees that grow seed-bearing fruit. These seeds will then produce the kinds of plants and trees from which they came." And that is what happened.

¹² The land produced vegetation—all sorts of seed-bearing plants, and trees with seed-bearing fruit. Their seeds produced plants and trees of the same kind. And God saw that it was good.

Genesis 1:11–12

1. WHATEVER YOU PLANT, YOU WILL REAP

A lot of us mess up here; we sow one thing and expect to receive another. But God clearly says that every seed produces fruit after its own kind. Ephesians confirms this:

"...knowing that whatever good anyone does, he will receive the same from the Lord...."

Ephesians 6:8a NKJV

This principle will never change. Genesis says:

As long as the earth remains, there will be planting and harvest, cold and heat, summer and winter, day and night.

Genesis 8:22

Sowing seed is how we activate God's command to be fruitful and multiply. We sow and it is multiplied back to us—the seed we sow bears fruit.

The seed principle is so powerful that even God isn't exempt from this law. God used the seed principle to bring his only begotten Son to earth; Jesus was a seed. In the *New King James Version* of the Bible in 1 Peter 1:23, it refers to Jesus as incorruptible seed. He was sown to reap a harvest of the redeemed.

Give what you want to receive. I am always trying to give away what I want to receive. Galatians reminds us:

Don't be misled—you cannot mock the justice of God. You will always harvest what you plant.

Galatians 6:7

Our grandson, God's faithful reward for the seeds we planted believing that God would bless our daughter and son-in-law with a baby.

For example, when I see someone pulled over by the police, I pray for them to receive favor and mercy. I ask God to let them off with a warning, and if I'm too late, I ask God to provide enough extra money to pay for the ticket. And I ask God to bless the police officer and keep him or her safe and protected. If John or I get pulled over, I say, "Lord, you said if I show mercy, I'll be given mercy. I need it now!" So far, so good!

What you make happen for others, God will make happen for you. When you do something for man, you will receive the reward from God. Notice it says that you reap *what* you sow not *where* you sow. That's an important aspect of giving. A few years ago, John and I really wanted grandchildren. Every time we heard of the birth of a baby, we bought a nice baby gift even if we barely knew the parents. In one week alone I bought gifts for four different expectant couples.

Then John and I went to Portland, Oregon, to visit our daughter and son-in-law. While we were there she took a pregnancy test. It was harvest time! We had the joy of being there when she learned she was pregnant. Not only that, but her doctor had told her she could not get pregnant and to get used to the idea of adoption. So much for that! A seed is so powerful it can break through anything.

2. DON'T SOW ALL YOUR SEED THE SAME WAY

God also wants us to diversify our giving. This was tough for me to learn. Once, John and I had legal troubles looming on the horizon. I asked God to show me where to plant seed to make the legal troubles disappear. I had a closet full of nice dress clothes I didn't need, and so I thought, "Here is some seed!" I quickly offered them to a Bible school student, but they weren't her size, so she politely turned them down.

Then I decided to give them to the clothing drive at church. They collect dress clothes for pastors' wives. I called our pastor's wife, Mary Jo, and told her I wanted to donate these nice clothes. She told me she felt I was to hang onto them!

I was baffled. God had prompted me to donate the clothes, but nobody would take them. I began to understand what it says in Isaiah:

> [26] The farmer knows just what to do, for God has given him understanding.
>
> [27] A heavy sledge is never used to thresh black cumin; rather, it is beaten with a light stick. A threshing wheel is never rolled on cumin; instead, it is beaten lightly with a flail.
>
> [28] Grain for bread is easily crushed, so he doesn't keep on pounding it. He threshes it under the wheels of a cart, but he doesn't pulverize it.
>
> [29] The LORD of Heaven's Armies is a wonderful teacher, and he gives the farmer great wisdom.
>
> **Isaiah 28:26–29**

In other words, the farmer knows that to get a harvest, he has to mix it up, do things differently, diversify his approach, and not just follow the same pattern for every different harvest. I confess that my first inclination is always to give to the church; I like to thresh all my crops the same way. But that is not Scriptural. Giving takes wisdom and discernment.

A little while later I was at a barbecue and, out of the blue, a woman told me that a local law school was looking for donated dress clothes for graduating law students so they could look good while interviewing for jobs.

Bingo!

Something leaped in my spirit. I called the school, and they came to my house and picked up the clothes. Our legal problems dissolved soon after that. In fact, our adversary paid us $8,000 to allow them to back out of the legal action.

I learned something from this experience. Seed must be planted in the right soil. God likes diversity of giving, and where we sow matters. I sowed to the law school and my legal troubles disappeared. I reaped what I had sown.

The other important lesson I learned was timing. I needed to be patient and wait for the right time. I was in a hurry to plant that seed because I felt like the problem was threatening, and I wanted it gone. But God will sometimes put that problem in a holding pattern while he works out all the details. Ecclesiastes says,

> [1] **For everything there is a season, a time for every activity under heaven.**
>
> [2] **...A time to plant and a time to harvest.**
>
> **Ecclesiastes 3:1–2b**

Sometimes, we must be patient and wait for that time.

3. SEED SHOULD BE SCATTERED

Our pastor, Dave Williams, teaches that smart investors diversify by planting multiple investments to receive multiple streams of income. This is a parallel truth: There are also multiple streams of income you can receive from investing in the Kingdom of God. Ecclesiastes tells us:

> [1] **Send your grain across the seas, and in time, profits will flow back to you.**
>
> [2] **But divide your investments among many places, for you do not know what risks might lie ahead.**
>
> [6] **Plant your seed in the morning and keep busy all afternoon, for you don't know if profit will come from one activity or another—or maybe both.**
>
> **Ecclesiastes 11:1–2, 6**

Proverbs confirms:

> **There is one who scatters, yet *increases more*; And there is one who withholds more than is right, But it leads to poverty.**
>
> **Proverbs 11:24, NKJV italics added**

You never know what a seed can do. You can count how many seeds are in an apple, but you can't count how many apples are in a seed! One seed actually contains an entire orchard because not only is the tree hidden within that seed the fruit is also hidden in the seed. And there are more seeds in that hidden fruit—see how it works? An entire orchard in one seed! That's potential!

God gives many fields in which to plant seed, but there is only one seed that gives supernatural return every time; that's the seed God specifically instructs you to plant. When God asks you to give, he already has in mind what your harvest will be—and it's always bigger than your seed. This miracle occurs when we plant under perfect conditions. For example, in Luke 5:2–11, Jesus asked Simon to "plant" his boat as a seed so that Jesus could preach from it. Simon got a huge supernatural harvest that same day, and went on to become a disciple.

I was at a Christian conference, sitting halfway back in this giant room. A well-known evangelist was to speak later in the week. I adore his ministry, so I cried out to God, "I want to sit in the front row when he speaks." Only a minute later, God answered my prayer. At the time, I didn't know he was answering it, but I felt prompted, "Give your special luncheon ticket to the woman next to you." So I asked her if she planned to go to the luncheon, and she told me she wanted to go but she didn't have a ticket. I said, "Well, you have one now!" She took it gladly.

She happened to be an usher, and she said, "These aren't exactly the best seats in the house, but I'll save you a seat right next to me for every service. You won't have to stand in line or anything." When I came into the giant room for the afternoon service that first day, she was not where I last saw her; she was flagging me down—from the front row! I sat front and center that night, and at every service the entire week.

If God ever asks you to plant a specific seed, plant it with great expectation because God already has your harvest on his mind. What could be more perfect sowing conditions than that?

4. DISCERN THE SEED

The Bible says God gives seed for sowing and bread for food. Once, I was flying with John and we were upgraded to first class—sweet!—but the seats were not together. As we walked down the jet-way, a soldier in uniform was in line in front of us. It was as if a light shone down on him; I wondered why. I felt prompted to talk to him, but the people ahead of him had his ear.

John and I turned toward first class and he turned toward coach, and that was that. We sat down in our separate seats, and both John's seat mate and mine refused to trade seats so we could be together. So here I was, stuck sitting next to a man who refused to move into the same seat, one row over. Awkward!

Suddenly I realized why that soldier was highlighted—I was supposed to offer my first class ticket to him to honor him. I had just eaten my seed for sowing! Heaven only knows the blessing I missed. If I could have kicked myself in the butt, I would have! I did not discern the seed so I consumed it.

5. INCREASE THE GIVING AS THE SEED INCREASES

Some people know how to sow and reap, but they never move higher in their receiving because they never move higher in their giving. A lot of regular tithers seem to fall into this category. There is a pattern you can get into of giving just ten percent and no more. The tithe is good and biblical. It establishes you in the covenant blessing of God, but it does not increase you. It is a starting point—not an ending point.

There are levels of progression in receiving, and we have to sow our way up: first the leaf, then the blade, and then the stalk. If I keep giving ten percent, how can I expect to move to greater return? I have heard many people who give ten percent pray for a hundred-fold return. What about the thirty and sixty-fold return Jesus talked about in Mark 4:8? We have to work our way up the ladder of progression. If we pray for a hundred-fold return, we have to give a hundred-fold offering, not simply the basic level tithe.

Sometimes people who tithe will get excited and give a little extra. They get an unusual harvest from it because God is faithful—he bumps them up to another level of return. But after they get the big harvest, they go right back to giving their usual ten percent, and they move themselves right back down to the ten-fold return. Their stay at the higher level lasted just a short time.

In order to move consistently out of the ten-fold return, you must consistently give more than ten percent of your income. You move up by increasing the percent you give. You never have to go back to the ten percent level. Keep moving forward! God said the measure you use will be measured back to you.

Once, John and I needed some big things, so we increased our giving by 50 percent. Only then did things start moving forward for us again. Don't wait for more money before you give a bigger measure. Use faith!

> **Yes, you will be enriched in every way so that you can always be generous.**
>
> **2 Corinthians 9:11a**

The people I know who have experienced advancement in their lives are consistently big givers. They give away hilariously, until the reaper overtakes the plowman. They give from their hearts like Abraham did. They don't keep records of God's generosity or hold him to account. Rather, they give cheerfully, from a heart full of love.

6. NAME THE SEED

Do you know that seed needs to be given instructions? You must plant purposefully and name your seed. Until you name your seed, there will be no harvest.

In 2 Kings 4:8–17, the woman from Shunem gave and gave, but she did not name her seed. She had not received a harvest from all her giving. However, that giving put her on Elisha's heart, and he asked her what she wanted. She replied, "Nothing." She didn't want to name her seed, but that seed was crying out for an instruction so Elisha named it for her. It's interesting that someone else can name your seed for you! Only after that seed was named did she get her harvest.

In 2 Chronicles 1:6–13, Solomon gave a thousand burnt offerings at the altar—but didn't name his seed. So God appeared to Solomon in a dream that very night and reminded him to name his seed. That's when Solomon asked for wisdom.

Do you see how important it is to plant with purpose? Name your seed and that is what you will reap.

7. WATER THE SEED WITH THE WORD OF GOD

The Bible says in Joel:

> **The seeds die in the parched ground, and the grain crops fail. The barns stand empty, and granaries are abandoned.**
>
> **Joel 1:17**

Sowing involves seed, time, and harvest. The "time" part is your opportunity to water your seed so it doesn't dry up. How do you water it? Speak the Word of God over your seed. Speak life and faith over it. Let the Word of God that dwells richly in your heart come out of your mouth. Speaking over the seed keeps your faith up and discouragement down.

Sow seeds of life into your own heart by spending time in the Word. When you plant God's Word in your heart it will produce God's life—and God is rich, rich, rich! Proverbs says,

> [20] My child, pay attention to what I say. Listen carefully to my words.
>
> [21] Don't lose sight of them. Let them penetrate deep into your heart,
>
> [22] for they bring life to those who find them, and healing to their whole body.
>
> **Proverbs 4:20–22**

It is not for nothing that the Word of God is often referred to in Scripture as "water." It is the water that brings our harvest to life.

In the next chapter I want to share additional "seed" principles that very few people understand, and no one talks about—even though they are crucial to giving in a way that takes us to new levels in Christ.

"Anyone can count the seeds in an apple, but only God can count the number of apples in a seed."

Robert H. Schuller

By planting my time into a place that had something
I wanted, I received the biggest harvest of my life…John!
Upward giving works!

CHAPTER 5

UPWARD GIVING—THE KEY TO ADVANCEMENT

I am about to share some principles I believe are meant for God's millionaire remnant the people with ears to hear what God says about seedtime and harvest. I believe those who embrace these principles will step forward into God's covenant of wealth. The principle is called "upward giving." I've found it's the fastest pathway to prosperity I know.

Picture a homeless man…you can almost hear those few coins clinking around the bottom of his empty McDonald's cup. "Can you spare some change?" he asks. Can you? Of course you can. I'm guessing your usual response would be to reach down in your pocket and toss in the leftover change from the bill you broke to buy your morning coffee. You probably wouldn't think twice about it. Why would you? Giving to the poor just comes naturally. That's just what we do—we give to non-profit organizations, missionaries, Goodwill, church offerings. We give an extra dollar while checking out at the grocery store in support of the local soup kitchen. It's not complicated; Christians and non-Christians alike give to those in need.

Thank God for that.

Here's a question for you: Have you ever given money to a wealthy man?

Now, picture a rich man: He's well dressed, has a nice car, a beautiful wife, and a beautiful home; he has all the "things" you would expect a wealthy man to have. Have you ever considered him when thinking of where to diversify your investments? Never? Even the thought of doing so is mind-boggling! I know what you're thinking: Why on God's green earth would I ever give my hard earned money or my precious time and energy to someone who doesn't need it—someone who already has everything he has ever wanted?

Because he has something you want. Upward giving is your vital connection to receiving what he has.

Have you ever wondered why God chose Abraham to be the father of many nations? I have. Why Abraham? What was it about him that got God's attention? I want to cultivate those same qualities, so I asked God what they were, and I believe his answer revealed one of the mysteries in the Bible. It is also the fastest path to prosperity that I know. This mystery is called "upward giving." Pastor Dave calls upward giving a "miracle covenant connection." He is so eloquent!

The concept is simple: Sow up to go up! Purposefully plant seed upward into fertile soil. Why? Before I explain the why, I want you to keep in mind these three statements as you read the explanation:

1. Giving is a covenant connector.

2. The seed connects you to the harvest.

3. The seed and the harvest both need the soil.

SOW UP TO GO UP

Sow up to go up means to plant seeds into the higher levels you want to attain. According to my study of Scripture, the most fertile soil of all is the man or woman of God, usually the pastor, priest, bishop, or teacher. When you give to a godly person, your seed connects you to the anointing on that person's life and forms a channel to bring that same anointing into your life. Those same abilities begin to flow in you, because giving is a covenant connector.

Remember, this is a spiritual concept—it's difficult to make total sense of it in the natural. The world says, "Take all you can, and give nothing back." God says, "Give, and it will be given." Let me show you what I mean through the example of Abraham.

By the last verse of Genesis 14, Abram was already called "wealthy" and had the promise. But the promise hadn't manifested. Then, suddenly, God appeared to Abram and gave him the covenant, that made him our spiritual father. What caused God to move this way at this particular moment? The answer: It was Abram's actions at a crucial seed-planting moment. Look at Genesis:

> ¹⁸ **And Melchizedek, the king of Salem and a priest of God Most High, brought Abram some bread and wine.**
>
> ¹⁹ **Melchizedek blessed Abram with this blessing:**
>
> **"Blessed be Abram by God Most High, Creator of heaven and earth.**
>
> ²⁰ **"And blessed be God Most High, who has defeated your enemies for you." Then Abram gave Melchizedek a tenth of all the goods he had recovered.**
>
> ²¹ **The king of Sodom said to Abram, "Give back my people who were captured. But you may keep for yourself all the goods you have recovered."**

> [22] **Abram replied to the king of Sodom, "I solemnly swear to the LORD, God Most High, Creator of heaven and earth,**
>
> [23] **"that I will not take so much as a single thread or sandal thong from what belongs to you. Otherwise you might say, 'I am the one who made Abram rich.'"**
>
> **Genesis 14:18–23**

Whoa! Hold up. Abram gave Melchizedek a tenth of everything? That was huge. Let's have another look at how this played out: When Sodom's king offered Abram his goods, Abram said, "No thanks; I don't want us to be connected." He would not accept seed from the king of a wicked people. That would have been a negative connection for sure. But immediately before that, Abram said, "I do want to be connected to you, Melchizedek, so I'm giving you ten percent of all I recovered." Abram practiced upward giving! Melchizedek didn't need the offering. However, Abram wanted to connect to Melchizedek's anointing, so he gave him ten percent.

Here's the amazing truth: When Abram gave upward, God had to move in his life—he had no choice—because giving is a covenant connector. God provided the fertile soil for Abram to sow into, but it wasn't until Abram seized the opportunity that the seed principle was activated. Since Melchizedek was a priest of the most high God, Abram actually became connected to Jesus through his upward giving. God even changed Abram's name to Abraham, giving Abraham part of God's name to show the world they were connected.

What did Abraham gain? God promised him as many descendants as stars in the sky, and great wealth for himself and his descendants. Abraham shot up to another level of living when he gave upwardly to Melchizedek. Why is this worthy of our attention? Because Ezekiel tells us:

> ...For what God has said applies to everyone—it
> will not be changed!
>
> **Ezekiel 7:13b**

That means you, too, can move God's hand with your upward giving. Abraham is your example. Hebrews adds to our understanding of this historical meeting:

> **⁶ But Melchizedek, who was not a descendant
> of Levi, collected a tenth from Abraham. And
> Melchizedek placed a blessing upon Abraham, the one
> who had already received the promises of God.**
>
> **⁷ And without question, the person who has the
> power to give a blessing is greater than the one who
> is blessed.**
>
> **Hebrews 7:6–7**

When you give upwardly you connect to someone at a higher level than yourself. It's like hitching your wagon to a star. God uses the upward giving principle to take you from glory to glory, as he has promised to do.

Hebrews also says:

> **So if the priesthood of Levi, on which the law
> was based, could have achieved the perfection God
> intended, why did God need to establish a different
> priesthood, with a priest in the order of Melchizedek
> instead of the order of Levi and Aaron?**
>
> **Hebrews 7:11**

Abraham wasn't the only one in this situation who had a need. God had a need! He needed to establish a different priesthood, and needed someone on earth to anchor it down by connecting to it. To fulfill God's ultimate plan you need to connect to that higher anointing. This is not about grabbing for what's best for you; it's about maturing in Christ to new levels of responsibility and greater anointing. Like us,

Abraham needed some fertile soil, because the tithe was never going to take him where he wanted to go. So the soil was presented, and Abraham planted the seed into it.

In an instant, both God and Abraham received what they needed to move forward—a new priesthood was established upon the earth, and Abraham reaped a harvest so big it covered us too, because we are his descendants. Abraham's upward giving was what set it all in motion.

Abraham's giving got God's attention, and so does yours. Upward giving works!

Before I was a Christian, and before I even knew what upward giving was, I had a very powerful experience with it.

When I was a college student, studying Exercise Physiology, I attended a field trip to a state-of-the-art, cutting-edge health club in our town and was given a tour by Chris, the Director of Personal Training. Well, something leapt inside me when I saw what was being done in that health club; I called Chris the next day and told him I needed to get my foot in the door somehow. Chris thanked me for my interest and told me they had no money left in the budget to hire anyone. But I would not be denied! I offered to work for free; I told Chris that I would do any job he wanted—no charge. He replied, "Can you start Monday?"

They put me on the payroll within a couple weeks of my hire, when they learned I was a single mother paying a baby sitter to work for free.

I had them all scratching their heads; what I did made no sense to the natural mind. Why would a person in my position offer time—and money—to work for free?

Well, from that one act of upward giving, by planting my time into a place that had something I wanted, I received the biggest harvest of my life! Chris had a best friend named

John. Chris introduced us, and I fell madly in love. We were married and are still living happily ever after.

But that is not all I received. When it was time to hire a personal trainer, I was already lined up for the job. I ultimately ended up with the same position as Chris—Director of Personal Training—at another health club in town. It's a fulfillment of the biblical mystery of upward giving. Upward giving works!

CAREFUL CONNECTIONS

The connection principle of the seed is so powerful that you must be very careful what you connect to. In Genesis, God gives us the law of the seed:

> [11] Then God said, "Let the land sprout with vegetation—every sort of seed-bearing plant, and trees that grow seed-bearing fruit. These seeds will then produce the kinds of plants and trees from which they came." And that is what happened.
>
> [12] The land produced vegetation—all sorts of seed-bearing plants, and trees with seed-bearing fruit. Their seeds produced plants and trees of the same kind. And God saw that it was good.
>
> **Genesis 1:11–12**

This verse clearly states that seeds can only produce after their own kind. Again, Galatians confirms this principle:

> Be not deceived; God is not mocked: for whatsoever a man soweth, that shall he also reap.
>
> **Galatians 6:7 KJV**

In other words, the seed will connect you to the harvest. But what kind of harvest? Harvests can be good or bad. If it's a bad harvest, it's called "consequences," but it's still a harvest.

Remember, God promised you always reap what you sow! And there are some harvests you do not want in your life!

For example, Proverbs 22:8 (NKJV) says that if you sow iniquity, you will reap sorrow. Financially, if you sow to the poor you will reap poverty through the miracle of covenant connection. That's the opposite of upward giving; we'll call it "downward giving." You must prayerfully and carefully sow your seed—because you will reap the harvest you sow.

Let me make this clear: giving to the poor is noble and good. In fact it's a biblical command. We give to the poor out of compassion (Proverbs 29:7), to honor God (Proverbs 14:31), and to show God's mercy (Proverbs 21:13). Proverbs 14:21 says, "Blessed are those who help the poor."

But you should not lay hands on those alms and pray for a harvest, because that kind of prayer will connect you to poverty by way of the seed, since every seed produces after its own kind. You don't want a harvest of poverty. When you give to the poor, you should obediently give and walk away. It is a loan to the Lord, but it is not a planted seed. It is also an act of obedience to God's command to help the poor. Jesus said in Luke:

> **9 "And does the master thank the servant for doing what he was told to do? Of course not.**
>
> **10 "In the same way, when you obey me you should say, 'We are unworthy servants who have simply done our duty.'"**
>
> **Luke 17:9–10**

Some time ago, John and I were in Portland, Oregon, walking to a health club. A homeless person approached us and asked for ten dollars. Without hesitating, John reached into his pocket and gave him ten dollars, and we kept walking.

When we arrived at the health club, the desk clerk asked us for $30 for the daily guest fee. Right then the manager walked by, and the desk clerk asked her a question about the fee transaction. The manager looked at us and said, "Just go on in today; no charge." The desk clerk said to us, "You got lucky." But John and I knew we had given ten dollars and saved thirty! There are promised blessings for obedience.

God blesses those who give to the poor, but again, don't treat it as seed. In Matthew 6:1–4, when Jesus talked about giving to the poor, he specifically instructed you to give your alms in secret. Why? So the seed won't be connected to you. You are also told not to give your best to the poor. Leviticus says to leave the edges of your fields for the poor. The best crops do not grow on the edges.

> **"When you harvest the crops of your land, do not harvest the grain along the edges of your fields, and do not pick up what the harvesters drop. Leave it for the poor and the foreigners living among you. I am the LORD your God."**
>
> **Leviticus 23:22**

Now, look at Numbers; it explains that your first and best is reserved for the man or woman of God.

> **"I also give you the harvest gifts brought by the people as offerings to the LORD—the best of the olive oil, new wine, and grain."**
>
> **Numbers 18:12**

That's upward giving. And it's easy! God put your best, most fertile soil right under your nose when he gave you your man or woman of God. Upward giving is the key that unlocks the treasure God has for us.

Even though you are encouraged to give your alms (your downward giving) to the poor in secret, I can't find any examples in the Bible of upward giving done in secret. When you give upwardly, you want the recipients to know that you desire a connection to their anointing. You want that covenant connection to be established.

I had already practiced upward giving because the Lord had spoken to me about it in my prayer time. However, I was praying to learn how to advance to an even higher level of living. God instructed me to start giving a percentage of my income to my pastors, Pastor Dave and Mary Jo Williams, personally every month. God asked me to specify that it was a personal gift and not for ministry. Now I give them a card every month with money in it, and I never ask for anything. I tell them not to even send a thank you note, and I thank them for receiving my seed.

DON'T EXPECT ANYTHING

This is a very important principle: Do not sow your seed upward expecting anything from the man or woman who receives your offering. You give expecting God to connect you to the same blessing that godly person has. You pull on the anointing, not the person. Remember, the Bible states that, "Every good and perfect gift comes from above." Also, since upward giving is a personal gift, it is not tax deductible.

The Bible says that if you walk with fools, you will become foolish; if you walk with the wise you will become wise. So, how do you break your connection to the foolish and establish a connection to the wise? Through upward giving!

After about two years of upward giving without understanding the principle behind it, I heard a preacher say that not every gift is for the ministry. My curiosity was piqued, so I looked in the Bible and discovered that upward giving is taught repeatedly.

In the book of Matthew, Jesus referred to upward giving as the "Prophet's Reward." he said:

> **"If you receive a prophet as one who speaks for God, you will be given the same reward as a prophet. And if you receive righteous people because of their righteousness, you will be given a reward like theirs."**
>
> **Matthew 10:41**

By sowing into the prophet you receive the prophet's reward. The Message Bible puts it this way:

> **The smallest act of giving or receiving makes you a true apprentice.**
>
> **Matthew 10:41 MSG**

An apprentice is a person who is learning a trade. By planting seed into the life of someone who has what you want, you are learning to have it, too! For example, John and I needed more wisdom, so we started planting seed into a recognized wisdom teacher. Soon, people started asking John to sit on boards of banks, medical companies, health clubs, and so on. They sought John's wisdom. It came as a direct result of our sowing into a wisdom teacher.

There are a number of examples in the Bible of upward giving, revealing that it really works! Let me share a few to establish in your mind that this principle is real and necessary to receiving and owning all of God's blessings.

THE STORY OF RAHAB

Rahab hid Israel's spies because they were children of God. Because of her actions, the spies were spared from death. So she and her family were spared from death as a reward. She also became one of the children of Israel and ended up in the lineage of Jesus (Joshua 6:25). Upward giving works!

ABIGAIL AND NABAL

David was God's man, and Nabal refused to help him. But Nabal's wife Abigail knew better; she went behind her husband's back and helped David. Foolish Nabal died, but wise Abigail did not! Abigail became King David's wife (1 Samuel 25). Upward giving works!

THE SHUNEMITE WOMAN

The woman from Shunem continually gave to Elisha. She kept saying she didn't need anything, but seeds need to be named. Finally the man of God named her seed for her and she immediately began to reap. She treated Elisha like a son, and she got a son of her own! When her son got sick and died, Elisha raised him from the dead. When there was a famine in the land, Elisha forewarned her and she escaped it. When the famine ended, Elisha saw to it that she got her property back, plus all the lost wages from those seven years (2 Kings 4:8–36; 8:1–6). Upward giving works!

THE SAMARITAN WOMAN

The Samaritan woman gave Jesus a simple cup of water and was rewarded with a harvest of salvation. She sowed water and reaped Living Water! Nearly her whole village came to Jesus (John 4:7, 41–42). Upward giving works!

JESUS AND MARY

Mary gave Jesus expensive perfume for his feet. Right away, Satan said through Judas, "That money should have been used for the poor." Jesus let everyone know that not every gift is for the ministry. Mary helped prepare Jesus for his historic burial, and her name went down in history—we are still telling her story more than 2,000 years later (John 12:3–8). Upward giving works!

MARY AND LAZARUS

In John 11, when Lazarus had died Jesus saw Martha and, instead of attending to Lazarus, he said, "Go get Mary." Jesus saw Mary crying and was moved to action because Mary had earned a connection with him through her upward giving and Martha hadn't. Upward giving works!

SIMON PETER

Simon (Peter) let Jesus use his boat as a platform from which to preach to the people. He got a huge supernatural harvest that same day, and was promoted from fisherman to a fisher of men, a Disciple of Christ (Luke 5:2–4, 9). Upward giving works!

PAUL IN PRISON

Paul's disciples gave him money in prison and Paul said:

And this same God who takes care of me will supply all your needs from his glorious riches, which have been given to us in Christ Jesus.

Philippians 4:19

We can't claim the supply part of the verse without obeying the take care of the man of God part. Paul made it clear, before he promised them their needs would be met, that it was because they first took care of Paul himself (Philippians 4:14–19). Upward giving works!

A few years ago, an amazing couple came to Lansing to speak at our Club 52 group. The man noticed John's belt and mentioned that he liked it, so when they were leaving John took off his belt and gave it to him. They thought it was so funny; no one had ever given upwardly to them—especially not a belt!

Well, it seemed like that was the end of the story—but upward giving works! The next year when they returned to speak again, they called John to the platform, told the belt story, and gave him a gift. Throughout the course of the day, we met and exchanged contact information. A relationship developed, and they invited John to be a guest on their television show.

Later, when they were hosting a very influential guest in their city, they included us in the special dinner they had for him.

Because of our miracle covenant connection with this couple, John and I had the opportunity and honor of breaking bread in a private dinner with a very wealthy, internationally renowned pastor, teacher, and diplomat. I was excited to sit at his feet, but even more excited to give him a personal gift—to give upwardly into his life.

When I presented him with a check, I explained that I wanted to connect to his anointing through the miracle of upward giving. He looked incredulous, grabbed my hand, and exclaimed, "Who taught you this? Where did you learn this?" Then he looked at my husband and said, "John, you have a very wise wife!" Yes!

Well, from that act of upward giving, John and I fell into the favor pool! We were invited to breakfast with him the next morning, and later we sat at the front table during the meeting. At the end of the weekend, he invited my husband to the platform, called him his friend, gave him a book, and honored him in front of the entire assembly. But wait, there's more! When we parted, he gave us his personal e-mail address and personal cell phone number: ACCESS!

And it all started with a belt!

Remember the story I told about giving ten dollars to the poor in Portland, Oregon? That was a loan to God, and we were repaid twenty dollars. It was a blessing. But when we gave upwardly, we were ADVANCED! Upward giving works!

I have searched the Bible diligently, and cannot find one example of upward giving ever failing. So, sow up to go up! Give to the man or woman of God. Do it openly to establish that covenant connection. Then watch how God brings that anointing to you as well.

Upward giving works!

Problems and strife are blessing blockers that will sabotage your life.

CHAPTER

PROBLEM SOLVING AT HOME

We have noticed something troubling—some people are fantastic in business, but they behave very differently at home. Instead of having initiative, solving problems, and creating solutions, they become passive and afraid of tackling difficult relational or home management problems. They seem to lack competence or confidence to accomplish in their family what they accomplish every day in business. So they end up with a house full of strife.

You can be a problem solver all day at work, but if you're not solving problems at home, blessings won't come. Strife is a blessing blocker that will sabotage your finances. Strife entangles your life in thorns. The dictionary defines strife as, "angry or bitter disagreement over fundamental issues, conflict, and incompatibility." The Bible warns that where there is strife you will find every evil thing:

For wherever there is jealousy and selfish ambition, there you will find disorder and evil of every kind.

James 3:16

We want to share about an unfruitful time we experienced early in our marriage. We asked God, "Why isn't our harvest coming in?" He revealed it was getting caught up in thorns because of the strife in our home.

You see, we went through a short season of strife early in our marriage. It's the only time since we have been together that we didn't prosper. The source of the strife was my conversion—I got saved first, and tried to pull John into the kingdom by arguing with him about it. Bad idea.

One day God said, "Judy, I want to hit John in the face with a pie, but you won't get out of the way long enough for me to get a clear shot!" So, I purposed in my heart to move out of God's way and let him help us. I promised to agree with John about everything and let God work on him from the inside.

I was tested right away. Two days later John mentioned that even though Mount Hope was the church I had chosen, as the man of the house he wanted to pick the church we attended. I loved my church and pastor so much, but I was determined to agree with John. So I said, "That's fine. You pray about it and wherever God sends us I'll go."

In my heart I thought, "I'm telling on you!" I ran to God, climbed on his lap and said, "Did you hear my husband? You gave me Pastor Dave to be my spiritual leader, and I know you wouldn't plant me in one place and John another. But I promised 'no strife,' so will you handle this?"

That very Sunday we attended Mount Hope. In the middle of his sermon, Pastor Dave stepped down from the platform and came right up the aisle to John! He put his Bible in John's lap, put his arm around John and said, "Look at this Scripture. Isn't it good?" He made John feel like part of the church family. John never mentioned leaving again!

God told me I only had one job—love John. God promised to do the changing if I did the loving. We slowly started becoming one. And guess what? We started prospering again.

Now when we see other couples arguing, we look at each other and shake our heads and say, "Rookie mistake." We have learned—the hard way—that there is a trick to staying out of strife. It's called "agreement," and it's powerful.

HOW TO AGREE ALL THE TIME

Agreement is the opposite of strife. It is harmony and compatibility. Matthew says:

> **19 "I also tell you this: If two of you agree here on earth concerning anything you ask, my Father in heaven will do it for you.**
>
> **20 "For where two or three gather together as my followers, I am there among them."**
>
> **Matthew 18:19–20**

The prayer of agreement is the most powerful prayer on earth. When two people are in agreement, nothing can stop them! Remember the tower of Babel in Genesis? God said:

> **"Look!" he said. "The people are united, and they all speak the same language. After this, nothing they set out to do will be impossible for them!"**
>
> **Genesis 11:6**

Deuteronomy says:

> **How could one person chase a thousand of them, and two people put ten thousand to flight, unless their Rock had sold them, unless the LORD had given them up?**
>
> **Deuteronomy 32:30**

Amos says:

> Can two people walk together without agreeing on
> the direction?
>
> Amos 3:3

Ecclesiastes tells us:

> ⁹ Two people are better off than one, for they can
> help each other succeed.
>
> ¹⁰ If one person falls, the other can reach out and
> help. But someone who falls alone is in real trouble.
>
> ¹¹ Likewise, two people lying close together can
> keep each other warm. But how can one be warm
> alone?
>
> ¹² A person standing alone can be attacked and
> defeated, but two can stand back-to-back and conquer.
> *Three are even better, for a triple-braided cord is not
> easily broken.*
>
> Ecclesiastes 4:9–12, italics added

That triple-braided cord is you, your spouse, and the
Holy Spirit. What a blessing to have someone who will agree
with you! God said in Genesis 2:18 that it is not good for
man (humans) to be alone. Why? Because when we are alone
we have no one to agree with us. Ecclesiastes 4:10 says that
people who are alone when they fall are in real trouble.

In Luke, chapter 22, Jesus was alone in the garden of
Gethsemane; all his disciples fell asleep. I think it's possible
that a spirit of sleep came over them so they wouldn't be
able to agree with Jesus during his moment of weakness,
when he said:

> "Father, if you are willing, please take this cup of
> suffering away from me."
>
> Luke 22:42a

If his disciples had been awake, they would have all agreed with Jesus, and God would have had to honor it. That's how powerful agreement is.

To keep strife out, the trick is to stay in agreement, and the best way to do that is to say, "I'm sorry!" right away. You have to cut strife off at the pass. Be quick to say you're sorry when you are wrong, and slow to speak when you're right. John is better at the second part, and I'm better at the first part. John has more practice being right, and I have more practice being the one to say, "I'm sorry."

One night, we were taking our kids out to dinner, and when we arrived I glimpsed the kids in the back seat exchanging money. They explained they had a bet going to see how many times I would apologize on the way to dinner. My son guessed right: eight times. I guess practice makes perfect!

Over the years, John and I have developed a number of different ways to apologize. Some are comical, but all of them work when they are sincerely meant. I want to share a few with you; feel free to make them your own.

- **The Stephanie**: You might remember the old Bob Newhart show, specifically a character named Stephanie. She was spoiled and arrogant. If she was ever wrong, she would shrug her shoulders, avoid eye contact, and in a nonchalant way say, "Sorry, sorry, sorry." I became really good at this before I was born again. It was my first crack at apologizing.
- **The Donald**: This is utilized when John knows that words won't do it; he's going to have to buy his way out. The wallet comes out, and he asks

me, "OK, how much will it take for you to put this behind us?" Thanks, Mr. Trump!

- **The Get-Out-of-Jail-Free:** We learned this one from our little niece. She thought she could do any naughty thing she wanted, and if she said she was sorry there would be no consequences. It's completely void of any real repentance, and it sounds like this: "I'm really sorry!" Not!
- **The Jillian:** Our niece taught us this one, too; it's John's personal favorite. Jillian's parents warned her repeatedly, and she didn't obey. She pushed them too far, and as they were whisking her

Jillian with her brother, Ben.

away to be spanked, she exclaimed, "I'm ready to listen! I'm ready to listen!" John uses this one when I've already warned him about something, and he keeps doing it until he goes too far. Then he backpedals quickly saying, "I'm ready to listen! I'm ready to listen!" Nice try, John.

- **The Simon Birch**: This is when my transgression against John is so great, it's as if I've sinned against man and God. I look up to heaven and plead, "I'm SORRRRRRRRRY...; I'm SORRRRRRRRRY...."

- **Charm School**: John used this one recently. I went to bed without washing the make-up off my face, and when I woke up my loving husband said I looked like a "crack whore." I got indignant, and John looked adorably at me and said, "Honey, I love you." He was apologizing without actually saying it. I'll admit—it works.

- **The Teenager**: This is one to avoid, because it only makes disagreements worse. Imagine a teenager giving you their most insincere "Sorry!" It really means, "I'm saying I'm sorry, but you're going to have to deal with it, because I have no intention of changing!" Roll your eyes and sigh heavily to make it even more aggravating.

- **The Trifecta**: This one utilizes three forms of apology: "I'm sorry! I'm ready to listen! Have mercy!"

- **The Academy Award**: This one is for John to use on those days I'm being "unreasonable." I'll be mad at John, and he won't know what he did wrong. Often it's nothing at all. But being a sterling husband who wants to keep peace, he musters his most sincere apology and pours his inner thespian into every word. The amazing thing is he never really knows what he's apologizing for; he should win an academy award for his acting. That doesn't matter to me. Sometimes you just want to hear it.

- **The Machine Gun**: I use this one when I offend John and immediately see the look on his face revealing that I've gone too far. Rapid-fire I unleash on him, "I'm sorry I'm sorry I'm sorry!"

- **The Toddler**: When I do something childish, like stepping on the back of his heel when we're walking, I'll put my finger in my mouth and say, "I sorry." Sometimes you just feel like a kid.

- **The Hail Mary**: This is John's last-ditch effort when all else has failed to bring forgiveness: He falls to his knees at my feet, clasps his hands together in the prayer position, and pleads in a desperate voice, "Mercy! I need mercy!"

There you have it—a dozen instant apology tools. I hope one or more of those help you to keep strife out of your home. Apologizing can be fun—try it!

PROTECTION AND PROSPERITY

There are more serious reasons to avoid strife. Our covenant with Jesus includes protection, but not if you get into strife and decide to fight your own battles. At those times, God will step back and let you defend yourself, for better or worse. Apart from the Vine you can do nothing, so it's always for worse.

The Bible says, in 1 Peter 2:23, that Jesus never defended himself but trusted the one who judges justly. Jesus didn't retaliate; he let God take care of it. That's your pattern for success.

Once, I was with John and my daughter Amber at the airport. We had just landed, and Amber and I were talking as we sauntered toward the tram. John was on his cell phone lagging behind. We were just about to step onto the tram when the doors closed. Directly behind us stood another traveler who was evidently in a huge hurry. When the doors closed, he started berating us. But I knew something he didn't—my husband was right behind him.

I knew I wouldn't have to fight this battle. John saw what was happening, dropped his phone, tapped the guy on the shoulder and said, "That's my wife! You don't talk to her that way!"

The guy whined, "They made me miss the train."

John sneered, "Ohhhhh! Boo hoo! Did that ruin your day?" They argued a minute more, and then John took his backpack off to let the man know he wasn't playing. The man slunk away.

My goodness! I was impressed! I had never seen that side of John—he was in protective love mode. How much more does God want to protect you? You are "the apple of his eye." No one had better pick a fight with you. If they do, I pity the fool!

Your job is simply to trust God. That means keeping your hands clean. Did you notice I never said a word to that man at the airport? I didn't have to. John jumped right in to defend me. That taught me a valuable lesson—back off and let God fight your battles. Now when someone does me wrong, I don't retaliate—I tell on them! Without telling anyone else first, I go to my Heavenly Father; I climb up on his lap and squeal on them. I tell my Dad all about it. He takes care of it for me, and he always knows just what to do, because he has all the facts. He is the Righteous Judge.

Get this fact in your head and it will change your life: "Don't mess with me—I don't fight my own battles."

I remember an occasion when some people did me wrong, so I ran to God, climbed up on his lap and said, "Dad, did you see what those people did to me? That really hurt."

God replied, "I saw it, and I will take care of it."

I got excited and asked, "What are you going to do to them?"

God said, "Nothing."

My heart sank. "Nothing? Didn't you just say you'd take care of it?"

He said, "I did, and I will."

I thought for a minute and asked, "How?"

God said, "I'm going to bless you so much, they're going to gnash their teeth when they see how you prosper!"

I learned another major lesson: There is a connection between protection and prosperity. Psalm 112:1–9 describes how blessed and prosperous the righteous will be. Then verse 10 says:

> **The wicked will see it and be grieved; He will gnash his teeth and melt away; The desire of the wicked shall perish.**
>
> **Psalm 112:10 NKJV**

That's protection in the midst of prosperity. They go hand-in-hand. God promises in Psalm 23 to prepare a table for you in the presence of your enemies. Again, protection and prosperity are paired.

Once, I was fighting with my sisters and said something I knew would make them gnash their teeth with jealousy. Realizing I had done wrong, I went off by myself and told God, "I repent. I shouldn't have done that."

His reply amazed me: "Haven't I done a good job of blessing you before the watching world? You just keep your hands clean and let me take care of everything." I love that God didn't scold me. He didn't say, "Don't do that!" He said, "Let me do that for you." He took me to Psalms:

> **How great is the goodness you have stored up**
> **for those who fear you. You lavish it on those who**
> **come to you for protection, blessing them before the**
> **watching world.**
>
> **Psalm 31:19**

Praise God! He is our Protector, our Source of prosperity, and our Master problem solver. However, there is one problem you face in life that can only be solved by you. Please read on to discover the path to the ultimate solution.

John and I rejoice in our faith.

CONCLUSION

SOLVING LIFE'S BIGGEST PROBLEM

There is a problem so big, so ominous, that no human can solve it for you. It's a problem every person is born into, and there is only one solution—only one way out!

John and I are unashamed of our faith in God, and feel we would be doing you a disservice if we didn't share with you the opportunity someone shared with us years ago.

You see, God created us—we are his creation—and he gave the rules and instructions for his creation.

> [26] Then God said, "Let us make human beings in our image, to be like us. They will reign over the fish in the sea, the birds in the sky, the livestock, all the wild animals on the earth, and the small animals that scurry along the ground."
>
> [27] So God created human beings in his own image. In the image of God he created them; male and female he created them.
>
> [28] Then God blessed them and said, "Be fruitful and multiply. Fill the earth and govern it. Reign over the

fish in the sea, the birds in the sky, and all the animals
that scurry along the ground."

Genesis 1:26–28

Laws cannot be broken without consequences. For example, if you jump from the fourteenth story of a skyscraper, God's law of gravity says you're going to die!

Just as there are natural laws God gave us moral laws, too. The problem is we've all violated them in some way. If we've ever gossiped, told a lie, dishonored our parents, used the Lord's name in cursing, or stolen a pen from the office we've broken God's Laws.

For everyone has sinned; we all fall short of God's glorious standard.

Romans 3:23

3 "You must not have any other god but me.

4 "You must not make for yourself an idol of any kind or an image of anything in the heavens or on the earth or in the sea.

5 You must not bow down to them or worship them, for I, the Lord your God, am a jealous God who will not tolerate your affection for any other gods. I lay the sins of the parents upon their children; the entire family is affected—even children in the third and fourth generations of those who reject me.

6 But I lavish unfailing love for a thousand generations on those who love me and obey my commands.

7 "You must not misuse the name of the Lord your God. The Lord will not let you go unpunished if you misuse his name.

8 "Remember to observe the Sabbath day by keeping it holy.

9 You have six days each week for your ordinary work,

[10] but the seventh day is a Sabbath day of rest dedicated to the Lord your God. On that day no one in your household may do any work. This includes you, your sons and daughters, your male and female servants, your livestock, and any foreigners living among you.

[11] For in six days the Lord made the heavens, the earth, the sea, and everything in them; but on the seventh day he rested. That is why the Lord blessed the Sabbath day and set it apart as holy.

[12] "Honor your father and mother. Then you will live a long, full life in the land the Lord your God is giving you.

[13] "You must not murder.

[14] "You must not commit adultery.

[15] "You must not steal.

[16] "You must not testify falsely against your neighbor.

[17] "You must not covet your neighbor's house. You must not covet your neighbor's wife, male or female servant, ox or donkey, or anything else that belongs to your neighbor."

Exodus 20:3–17

Why do these sins matter? Because one sin—that's right even one little sin—will keep you out of heaven and away from God's favor.

For the person who keeps all of the laws except one is as guilty as a person who has broken all of God's laws.

James 2:10

Gaining God's favor is important because his favor has the power to make you wealthy and successful.

> **The blessing of the Lord makes a person rich,
> and he adds no sorrow with it.**
>
> **Proverbs 10:22**

> **Remember the Lord your God. He is the one who
> gives you power to be successful, in order to fulfill the
> covenant he confirmed to your ancestors with an oath.**
>
> **Deuteronomy 8:18**

We know there are many who are rich in this life, yet have no use for God. However, "What does it profit a man if he gains the whole world, then loses his soul?"

Our pastor, Dave Williams, calls hell "the garbage dump of the universe." And Jesus said it was never created for people, but for demons. Yet people who do not have a Savior must go there to live for eternity with no bail, no bond, and no hope…forever separated from God without a prayer. Sometimes we've heard hell called "the dungeons of the damned."

But the good news is, God loves you too much to leave you without hope. So God gave you a choice: Pay for your own sins by going to hell, or use a substitute to pay for your sins. God even provided the substitute—Jesus. He sent his only begotten son, Jesus Christ, to save you from your sins. Jesus gave you the perfect gift that only he could give. Only if you accept his payment will you know God's favor on your life now and have a home in heaven in the next life.

Jesus was conceived of the Holy Spirit, born of the Blessed Virgin, Mary, and lived a sinless life—fully man, yet fully God. He went around doing good things for people and healing all who were sick and oppressed.

In spite of all the good Jesus did, and his amazing and practical teaching, the jealous religious leaders convinced the

Romans to execute him on a cross outside of Jerusalem. Jesus was innocent but still he suffered and died. As he was dying, all the sins of the world: past, present, and future were placed on him. Then a miracle occurred! After three days, he rose from the dead and talked with over 500 people. Jesus then ascended to heaven, and he sits by God the Father interceding on our behalf. Before he left, Jesus promised he would come back again.

Now, if we accept God's payment for our sins, all our sins travel back in time to Jesus when he hung on the cross. And all his righteousness travels forward and is imputed unto us. We become children of God by receiving the payment for our sins, and the payment is a Person—none other than God's Son, Jesus Christ! It's God's only plan—there is no "Plan B" to get us into heaven.

There is only one requirement to receiving this perfect gift: We have to ask. It's very humbling to admit that we are sinful, and many people find it difficult to ask for help.

That's where the problem solvers come in! We know a prayer you can pray, right now, wherever you are, and God will wash all your sins away, welcome you into his family, and give you a home in heaven.

It sounds too good to be true, doesn't it? We know! You don't have to understand it all, but you do have to believe, and trust that understanding will come in time.

Just pray this prayer from your heart:

Dear God,

Please forgive me of all my sins. I have fallen short of your standards, and accept your payment for my sins. I believe Jesus is the eternal Son of God. I believe he died on the cross for my sins, and I believe he was raised from the dead. Right now, I ask Jesus to come into my heart, give me a new nature, and write my name in Heaven's Book of Life.

God, you are now my Heavenly Father, Protector, and Provider. Thank you for receiving me as your child. Please fill me with your Holy Spirit, and help me find a great Bible-believing church. Thank you, Father. I declare now: I am forgiven; I am saved; I have a home in Heaven and a brand new start in life.

Amen.

Congratulations! Welcome to God's family! Now that you are a child of God, there's one thing you can do! You can tell other people that Jesus saved your soul! Tell someone today, okay? Tell them you have a new Father, and he is so proud of you—he even has your picture in his wallet! He loves you! Tell them God is preparing a mansion for you in heaven even now. And tell them it's because Jesus died for you. Isn't that good news? God bless you!

To wrap things up, in this book we have talked about how to:

- Make problem solving the focus of your life in all areas
- Let God become your problem solver and learn to receive from him
- Master the seed principle
- Sow up to go up by learning upward giving
- Allow your heavenly Daddy to solve your problems and fight your battles

Each of these principles are powerful and will help you find a sure path to the riches and blessings God has prepared especially for you. We are living proof that he is faithful to do it. Read this book, or specific parts of it, as many times as you need to get it into your spirit.

Now, go and be blessed!

If you prayed that prayer and want help in your spiritual journey, send for a free copy of Dave Williams' bestselling book, *The New Life...the Start of Something Wonderful*. Please write to: Decapolis Publishing, P.O. Box 80825, Lansing, MI, 48908-0825.

"Become a fixer, not just a fixture."

Anthony J. D'Angelo

RECOMMENDED READING

1. Guyon, Jeanne. *Experiencing God Through Prayer*: Whitaker House Publishers, 1030 Hunt Valley Circle, New Kensington, PA, 15068, 2000.

2. Harrison, Bob. *Power Points for Increase*: Harrison House Publishers, P.O. Box 35035, Tulsa, OK, 74153, 2010.

3. Munroe, Myles. *Becoming a Leader*: Whitaker House Publishers, 1030 Hunt Valley Circle, New Kensington, PA 15068, 1993.

4. Munroe, Myles. *God's Big Idea: Reclaiming God's Original Purpose for Your Life*: Destiny Image Publishers, Inc., P.O. Box 310, Shippensburg, PA, 17257, 2008.

5. Munroe, Myles. *Passing it On*: Faith Words, Hachette Book Group, 237 Park Ave., New York, NY, 2011.

6. Munroe, Myles. *Understanding the Purpose and Power of Prayer*: Whitaker House, 1030 Hunt Valley Circle, New Kensington, PA, 15068, 2002.

7. Murdock, Mike. *The Law of Recognition*: Wisdom International, 4051 Denton Highway, Ft. Worth, TX, 76117, 2001.

8. Murdock, Mike. *The Wisdom Commentary of Mike Murdock, Vol. 1*: Wisdom International, 4051 Denton Highway, Ft. Worth, TX, 76117, 2003.

9. Thompson, Leroy. *Becoming a Commander of Covenant Wealth*: Ever Increasing Word Ministries, P.O. Box 7, Darrow, LA, 70725, 2005.

10. Thompson, Leroy. *How to Find Your Wealthy Place*: Ever Increasing Word Ministries, P.O. Box 7, Darrow, LA, 70725, 1999.

11. Thompson, Leroy. *I'll Never be Broke Another Day in My Life*: Ever Increasing Word Ministries, P.O. Box 7, Darrow, LA, 70725, 2001.

12. Thompson, Leroy. *Money Cometh!*: Ever Increasing Word Ministries, P.O. Box 7, Darrow, LA, 70725, 1997.

13. Thompson, Leroy. *Money Thou Art Loosed*: Ever Increasing Word Ministries, P.O. Box 7, Darrow, LA, 70725, 1999.

14. Thompson, Leroy. *No More Empty Hands!*: Ever Increasing Word Ministries, P.O. Box 7, Darrow, LA, 70725, 2008.

15. Thompson, Leroy. *You're Not Broke You Have a Seed*: Ever Increasing Word Ministries, P.O. Box 7, Darrow, LA, 70725, 2003.

16. Williams, Dave. *Coming Into the Wealthy Place*: Decapolis Publishing, 202 S. Creyts, Lansing, MI, 48917, 2004.

17. Williams, Dave. *How to Help Your Pastor Succeed*: Decapolis Publishing, 202 S. Creyts, Lansing, MI, 48917, 2005, 2008.

18. Williams, Dave. *Miracle Breakthrough Power of the First Fruit*: Decapolis Publishing, 202 S. Creyts, Lansing, MI, 48917. 2008.

19. Williams, Dave. *The Pastor's Pay*: Decapolis Publishing, 202 S. Creyts, Lansing, MI 48917, 1989, 2010.

20. Williams, Dave. *The Road to Radical Riches*: Decapolis Publishing, 202 S. Creyts, Lansing, MI, 48917, 2000.

About Judy O'Leary:

Judy O'Leary is a graduate of Mount Hope Church Bible Training Institute and also holds a Bachelor of Science Degree in Exercise Physiology from Michigan State University. She is certified as a Strength and Conditioning Specialist and Personal Trainer, with over 10 years experience. As Director of Personal Training, she increased sales 500% her first year and spoke on a variety of health related and spiritual topics in the community.

John and Judy have three children, one son-in-law, and one grandchild. They live in East Lansing, Michigan, and attend Mount Hope Church.

About John D. O'Leary

John O'Leary holds a Bachelor of Business Administration from the University of Colorado. He is co-president of O'Leary Paint Company, the largest privately held architectural paint manufacturer in Michigan, distributing paint through their own network of stores. They are nationally recognized in the Top 40 paint dealers in North America.

John is:

- President, Board of Directors, AllPro Corporation (a national and international 20 member buying group managing over 260 million dollars in purchases)
- President, Executive Board Member, Coating Research Group, Inc. (an international group of paint manufacturers representing seven countries)
- Board of Directors; Chairman, Credit Risk Committee of Capitol National Bank
- Co-chairman of Local Initiatives Support Corporation

- Advisory Counsel (2003–2005) of Empty Plate Campaign supporting the Lansing Food Bank
- Advisory Counsel of Michigan Athletic Club
- Board of Directors of Medisiss Company (a surgical reprocessing company)

CONTACT INFORMATION

Decapolis Publishing
P.O. Box 80825,
Lansing, MI, 48908-0825
1-800-888-7284
www.decapolisbooks.com

MORE **LIFE CHANGING**
BOOKS FROM **DECAPOLIS PUBLISHING**

8⁹⁵

Your Spectacular Mind

Your thoughts create your environment. If you want a better life, you need better thinking. In this book, Dave Williams unlocks the mysteries of the mind, giving you plans and strategies for developing your mind—an awesome gift from God.

108 PAGES

12⁹⁵

Emerging Leaders

They are wall breakers and city takers! Don't try to stop them; they are unstoppable. They are EMERGING LEADERS—a new breed of church leadership for the 21st century, and you can be one of them!

168 PAGES

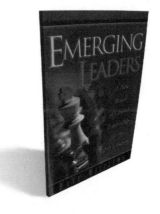

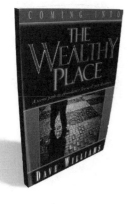

14⁹⁵

Coming Into The Wealthy Place

God wants you to be able to "abound to every good work." You need to learn how to release God's power in your life to get wealth. This book will show you how to go through the door of just good enough into *The Wealthy Place!*

170 PAGES